# SHAME-SEX ATTRACTION

of related interest

**Written on the Body**
Letters from Trans and Non-Binary Survivors of
Sexual Assault and Domestic Violence
*Edited by Lexie Bean*
ISBN 978 1 78592 797 3
eISBN 978 1 78450 803 6

**Gender Trauma**
Healing Cultural, Social, and Historical Gendered Trauma
*Alex Iantaffi*
*Foreword by Meg-John Barker*
ISBN 978 1 78775 106 4
eISBN 978 1 78775 107 1

**Uncomfortable Labels**
*Laura Kate Dale*
ISBN 978 1 78592 587 0
eISBN 978 1 78592 588 7

# SHAME-SEX ATTRACTION

## SURVIVORS' STORIES OF CONVERSION THERAPY

LUCAS F. W. WILSON

Foreword by Garrard Conley

**Jessica Kingsley Publishers**
London and Philadelphia

First published in Great Britain in 2025 by Jessica Kingsley Publishers
An imprint of John Murray Press

3

Copyright © Lucas F. W. Wilson 2025
Foreword Copyright © Garrard Conley 2025

The right of Lucas F. W. Wilson to be identified as the Author of the Work has been
asserted by them in accordance with the Copyright, Designs and Patents Act 1988.

Chapter 1 © Gregory Elsasser-Chavez, Chapter 2 © D. Apple, Chapter 3 ©
Peter Nunn, Chapter 4 © Chaim Levin, Chapter 5 © Jordan Sullivan, Chapter
6 © Nathan Xie, Chapter 7 © Lexie Bean, Chapter 8 © Megan Poirier, Chapter
9 © Kim Kemmis, Chapter 10 © Jonathon Sawyer, Chapter 11 © Chris Csabs,
Chapter 12 © Rick Danielson, Chapter 13 © Syre Klenke, Chapter 14 © Colin
Bland, Chapter 15 © Gemma Hickey, Chapter 16 © Tyler Krumland

This book contains mention of transphobia, homophobia, abuse and childhood abuse.

A CIP catalogue record for this title is available from the
British Library and the Library of Congress

ISBN 978 1 80501 132 3
eISBN 978 1 80501 133 0

Printed and bound in the United States by Integrated Books International

Jessica Kingsley Publishers' policy is to use papers that are natural, renewable and recyclable
products and made from wood grown in sustainable forests. The logging and manufacturing
processes are expected to conform to the environmental regulations of the country of origin.

Jessica Kingsley Publishers
Carmelite House
50 Victoria Embankment
London EC4Y 0DZ

www.jkp.com

John Murray Press
Part of Hodder & Stoughton Limited
An Hachette UK Company

The authorised representative in the EEA is Hachette Ireland,
8 Castlecourt Centre, Dublin 15, D15 XTP3, Ireland (email: info@hbgi.ie)

# CONTENTS

# FOREWORD

## GARRARD CONLEY

Perhaps you've heard the story by now. It takes place in a clinic, a pastor's office, a camp, a private university, round a dining room table, inside someone's head. In every telling, shame claims the starring role, a shame powerful enough to erase what it means to be human. There are the usual beats: humiliation and self-loathing, followed by the offer of a "cure"; cult-like rules and self-flagellation; the tendency toward self-harm and/or suicide; and finally, if the story is one of survival, the realization, the breaking point, the coming to terms with one's authentic self. That the stories of conversion therapy can easily shape their own genre should come as no surprise; the practice, no matter what dubious form it takes, is extremely formulaic. Its repetitive nature gives it its power, the same power all fundamentalist teachings possess. *It's simple,* conversion therapy says. All you must do is follow the rules, even if the rules shift with each new iteration, each crackpot theory, each therapist with a faulty Freudian interpretation.

In preparing to write this foreword, I spent several months poring over the essays in this collection, missing my deadline several times. Despite having shared my own conversion therapy story hundreds of times—in memoir and film and through speaking engagements, interviews, and my work as an activist—I was unprepared for the profound emotional impact of reading how these writers grappled with, and ultimately could not erase, an essential part of their identities. The genre I thought I knew so well suddenly became new to me. In ways I never could see in my own story, I witnessed the beauty and humanity within these individuals who were told they were anything but human and beautiful. I found myself enraged at those who failed to accept these individuals as they are, particularly those unable to navigate the nuanced gray areas that define so much of our humanity. This journey not only softened my heart but also illuminated the profound power of the personal essay, revealing depths I had not fully appreciated in my decade as a creative non-fiction professor.

When I first began writing *Boy Erased* in 2013, only two states in the U.S.—California and New Jersey—had banned this harmful practice. When you typed the words "conversion therapy" into a search engine, you were likely to find ads promoting the practice rather than dire warnings from lesbian, gay, bisexual, transgender, queer, Two-Spirit, and other sexual-minority and gender-nonconforming (LGBTQ2S+) organizations. I wrote my story from a lonely place, scouring the internet for any other survivors I could find, and what I often discovered in these raw accounts tended to trigger me. When I tuned into *Saturday Night Live* one night to take a break, I saw Ben Affleck making jokes—funny, I suppose, in the abstract—about how all conversion therapy counselors were secretly gay. But I couldn't laugh.

There was too much pain, too much silence. At the time, there were no clear numbers on how many people had shared this experience. Reading the essays in *Shame-Sex Attraction* helped me see that, despite our feelings of extreme isolation, we were never alone.

Each of us brings something unique to this emerging genre—one I hope will be short-lived, a dark historical artifact—but we also share a story of survival. The shame never quite goes away, and some of us live with it more than others, but we all live to tell the story. Though many essays have no clear resolution, I take comfort in the fact that these writers have all shaped their experiences into something truly enlightening. The very act of telling these stories serves as their resolution, offering the happiest ending imaginable—because once, not so long ago, our stories didn't even exist. I am profoundly grateful to these writers for preserving our collective history, sharing their darkest moments, and restoring my faith in the transformative power of storytelling.

# INTRODUCTION

## LUCAS F. W. WILSON

Over the past half century LGBTQ2S+ communities have increasingly gained civil rights and social acceptance. Through the painstaking work and persistence of countless advocates, LGBTQ2S+ communities have come to see the fruits of their labor in numerous areas, such as anti-discrimination legislation, the recognition of civil unions, marriage equality, positive media representations, access to appropriate healthcare, religious inclusion and ordination, and beyond. Of course, this upward trend has been neither easy nor linear, as these advancements have been—and possibly always will be—repeatedly challenged.

One particularly slow-moving aspect of LGBTQ2S+ liberation has been the fight against what is widely known as *conversion therapy*.[1] Conversion therapy—also referred to as

---

1    The term *conversion therapy*, though most likely recognizable to general audiences, is not always the preferred term when referring to change efforts. The term is a misnomer; there is no conversion involved in these sorts of practices—no individual has ever "converted" to straight or cisgender—nor do these practices possess any therapeutic value. The terms *conversion practices, conversion efforts,* or *sexual orientation and gender identity and expression change efforts (SOGIECEs)* are often used in lieu of *conversion therapy*. This is not to say that there is a consensus

*reparative, change, reintegrative, desistance, gender-exploration,* or *reorientation therapy*—constitutes the harmful practices, subtle or blatant, that attempt to alter LGBTQ2S+ individuals' sexual orientations, gender identities, and/or gender expressions in order to "achieve" heterosexuality and/or heteronormativity. In order to "attain" heterosexuality and heteronormativity—the so-called desired outcomes for those undergoing conversion practices—LGBTQ2S+ individuals are taught how to "repair," "reduce," or suppress their non-normative sexual desires and behavior and gender identities and expressions through various conversion practices. Conversion practices include, but can extend beyond, talk-therapy counseling, "support" groups and camps, transphobic healthcare practices, "corrective" prayer, forced celibacy, coerced sexual relations or relationships, behavioral suppression and "correction," aversion therapy, electroshock therapy, online programs, and exorcisms.[2] Such practices can be formal or informal and vary widely depending on the context and region in which they take place, though the

surrounding terminology—far from it. Regardless, individuals should use the term that makes most sense for them and their communities. Throughout this introduction, I alternate between using conversion therapy, conversion efforts, and conversion practices. (Some of this above information comes from a draft document prepared by Wisdom2Action, a social enterprise and consulting firm supporting civil society organizations and governments to facilitate change and strengthen communities. I received this document, entitled "Know Your Rights," when I was part of a Justice Canada-funded advisory committee, which was organized by Wisdom2Action after conversion therapy was banned in Canada. This document was never formally published, but I want to acknowledge where this information comes from.)

2    Jones, T. *et al.* (2022) "Religious conversion practices and LGBTQA+ youth." *Sexuality Research and Social Policy,* 19.

vast majority of these practices share an underlying ideology that wreaks immense harm on its victims.[3]

*Conversion ideology,* a term first used in Chris Csabs *et al.*'s "SOGICE Survivor Statement," names the beliefs and teachings that frame LGBTQ2S+ individuals as incomplete, broken, sick, and/or degenerate. These beliefs and teachings work in tandem with the underlying cultures of heteronormativity, as they posit that queers are not actually queer but are instead latent or potential heterosexuals who possess the ability to "reform" their sexualities and gender identities and expressions. According to this thinking, sexual and gender nonconformity are not intrinsic parts of queer subjects' personhoods, that is, not inherent or constitutive aspects of their subjectivities. The heteronormative standards that individuals are taught to adopt correspond with a binary understanding of gender that is based on the sex they are assigned at birth.[4]

In line with essentialist theories of gender and sexuality that undergird conversion practices, conversion ideology argues that "same-sex attraction"—the phrase commonly used to describe queer desire—and gender nonconformity are the result of certain root issues. These issues might include sexual

---

3   Csabs, C. *et al.* (2020) "SOGICE Survivor Statement, Version 4." Sydney and Melbourne: SOGICE Survivors and Brave Network.

4   Csabs, C. *et al.* (2022) "SOGICE Survivor Statement"; Jones, T. *et al.* (2021) "Mis-education of Australian youth: Exposure to LGBTQA+ conversion ideology and practices." *Sex Education,* 22(5); Sullivan, J., Archibald, R., and Kwag, M. (2022) "SOGIECE/CT Survivor Support Project: Findings from a national survey, focus groups, and interviews with hundreds of survivors, 2021–22." Community-Based Research Centre; Robinson, C. M. and Spivey, S. E. (2015) "Putting lesbians in their place: Deconstructing ex-gay discourses of female homosexuality in a global context." *Social Sciences,* 4.

abuse, a damaged or inadequate relationship with a parent or both parents, other damaged or inadequate family relationships, negative experiences with the opposite sex, pornography, negative spiritual influences (e.g., demonic possession), and/or a predatory member of the same sex. In identifying one or more of these root issues as the cause or causes for so-called same-sex attraction and gender nonconformity, conversion ideology gaslights LGBTQ2S+ individuals into denying the authenticity of their sexuality and/or gender—that is, rejecting the legitimacy of their queer identity and/or expression.[5] As the reality of their queerness is repudiated, victims of conversion practices are thus primed to conform to the heteronormative standards set out for them by conversion practitioners.[6]

The many practices that fall under the umbrella of conversion therapy have numerous damaging, death-dealing, and no doubt disastrous consequences. In a national Canadian study, the most common impact of conversion therapy was shame, followed by anxiety, difficulty celebrating LGBTQ2S+ identities, depression, difficulty in romantic and/or sexual relationships,

---

5    Robinson, C. M. and Spivey, S. E. (2015) "Putting lesbians in their place:
     Deconstructing ex-gay discourses of female homosexuality in a global context."
     Robinson, C. M. and Spivey, S. E. (2007) "The politics of masculinity and the
     ex-gay movement." *Gender and Society*, 21(5).

6    Here and elsewhere, I use the term *conversion practitioners*, instead of *conversion
     therapists*, because the term *conversion therapist* is a misnomer when applied
     broadly. There is a wide range of people in numerous settings who deliver
     conversion practices, not just those who are dedicated to a consistent, ongoing
     delivery of such practices in a counseling or pastoral setting (i.e., those common-
     ly thought of as conversion therapists). As such, although there are many who
     may appropriately be identified as conversion therapists, there are many who
     are not conversion therapists but are, instead, conversion practitioners.

isolation, poor self-esteem, self-loathing, disruption in family relationships, anger, and suicidal ideation.[7] Other research has found that undergoing conversion practices results in greater abuse of drugs and alcohol, loneliness, increased risk of experiencing homelessness, negative impacts on identity formation, and overall poorer mental health.[8] Because of the informal nature of many conversion practices, some survivors do not grasp that they are in fact survivors or that they may need particular kinds of support that survivors require. However, many survivors *have* expressed needing—and have sought out—psychological treatment, particularly for post-traumatic stress disorder, complex trauma, and/or post-religious trauma.[9] Despite how all reputable scientific literature and professional codes of ethics denounce conversion practices for the many harms they cause,[10] these practices endure, especially in religious spaces.

Though not all conversion therapy occurs in religious contexts—and despite how religious assertions about

7   Sullivan, J. *et al.* (2022) "SOGIECE/CT Survivor Support Project: Findings from a national survey, focus groups, and interviews with hundreds of survivors, 2021–22." Community-Based Research Centre.

8   Jones, T. W., Power, J., and Jones, T. M. (2022) "Religious trauma and moral injury from LGBTQA+ conversion practices." *Social Science & Medicine*, 305.

9   Anderson, J. R. *et al.* (2024) "Mental health practitioners' knowledge of LGBTQA+ conversion practices and their perceptions of impacts on survivors." *Journal of Homosexuality*; Despott, N. *et al.* (2023) *Supporting Survivors of LGBTQA+ Conversion Ideology and Practices: A Reference Guide.* Melbourne: La Trobe University; Anderson, J. R. *et al.* (2023) "Engaging mental health service providers to recognize and support conversion practice survivors through their journey to recovery." *Cognitive and Behavioral Practice*; Streed, C. G. *et al.* (2019) "Changing medical practice, not patients—putting an end to conversion therapy." *The New England Journal of Medicine*, 381(6).

10  Alempijevic, D. *et al.* (2020) "Statement on conversion therapy." *Journal of Forensic and Legal Medicine*, 72.

LGBTQ2S+ individuals are separate from pseudoscientific claims that employ psychological language to explain the root "causes" and "dysfunction" of LGBTQ2S+ identities and expressions[11]—a significant percentage of conversion practices take place at the hands of religious practitioners,[12] resulting in numerous dimensions of spiritual harm. Spiritual harms include damage to victims' spiritual self-identity, their ability to construct existential meaning, their relationship to God or the divine, and their relationship to their religious community. The two terms frequently employed in psychological literature to describe elements of spiritual harm are *religious trauma* and *moral injury*. Whereas religious trauma is caused by the coercive, manipulative, and abusive aspects of religion-based conversion practices—particularly the ongoing accumulation of derogatory messages[13]—moral injury is a result of learning about, observing, failing to stop, and/or being complicit in actions that violate deeply held moral beliefs.[14] Different from, but related to, religious trauma, moral injury is concerned with symptoms related to guilt, shame, anger, and disgust.[15] Victims

11  Jones, T. *et al.* (2022) "Religious conversion practices and LGBTQA+ youth." *Sexuality Research and Social Policy,* 19.

12  Salway, T. *et al.* (2019) "Protecting Canadian Sexual and Gender Minorities from Harmful Sexual Orientation and Gender Identity Change Efforts." A brief submitted to the Standing Committee on Health for the Committee's study of LGBTQ2 Health in Canada.

13  Jones, T. W. *et al.* (2022) "Religious trauma and moral injury from LGBTQA+ conversion practices." *Social Science & Medicine,* 305.

14  Litz, B. T. *et al.* (2009) "Moral injury and moral repair in war veterans: A preliminary model and intervention strategy." *Clinical Psychological Review,* 29(8).

15  Farnsworth, J. K. *et al.* (2014) "The role of moral emotions in military trauma: Implications for the study and treatment of moral injury." *Review of General Psychology,* 18(4). See also Jones, T. M. *et al.* (2022) "Supporting LGBTQA+

of conversion practices often experience moral injury when their sexual or gendered subjectivities are in conflict with their sincerely held moral beliefs and expectations. As they are forced to choose between these core parts of themselves and thus try to change or suppress their sexualities or genders in an effort to maintain their beliefs, they are witnesses to and personally implicated in—however coerced or manipulated they might be—their own moral failure.[16] Such is the insidious nature of religious conversion practices, which give rise to a multitude of spiritual harms.

Various studies have demonstrated the prevalence of conversion practices across national contexts. In Australia, 4% of LGBTQ2S+ young people aged 14–21 who were surveyed had experienced conversion practices.[17] A U.K. survey revealed that 7% of LGBTQ2S+ British adults were encouraged to undergo conversion practices, with 2% eventually following through. For specific minority populations, these numbers staggeringly rose to between 13% and 44%. In Canada, similar findings have demonstrated that Indigenous, intersex, transgender, non-binary, and asexual persons, people of color, as well as individuals whose sexual orientation is not monosexual (i.e., bisexual, pansexual, etc.) were much more likely to have been exposed to conversion practices.[18] One study found that 4% of

peoples' recovery from sexual orientation and gender identity and expression change efforts." *Australian Psychologist*, 57(6).

16   Jones, T. W. *et al.* (2022) "Religious trauma and moral injury from LGBTQA+ conversion practices." *Social Science & Medicine*, 305.

17   Ibid.

18   Blais, M. *et al.* (2022) "Sexual orientation and gender identity and expression conversion exposure and their correlates among LGBTQI2+ persons in Québec,

all sexual minority men in Canada have been exposed to conversion practices, but work by leading experts suggests this is an underestimate, especially when considering the 7% of sexual and gender minority adults in the U.S. who have been exposed to conversion practices.[19] Other surveys in Global North contexts have indicated that approximately 8% of respondents had undergone formal conversion practices.[20] But it is worth underscoring how the statistics are possibly, in reality, higher. This is because of the problem of self-reporting. Many who have undergone conversion practices may not have participated in the aforementioned surveys (especially if they are still a part of a religious community, particularly those that distrust scientific and medical findings). Moreover, many respondents may not in fact know if they underwent change efforts, as they may have not considered their experiences as falling under the umbrella of conversion therapy. In either case, the number of individuals who have undergone conversion practices is one too many.

---

Canada." *PLoS ONE*, 17(4); Salway, T. *et al.* (2021) "Experiences with sexual orientation and gender identity conversion therapy practices among sexual minority men in Canada, 2019–2020." *PLoS ONE*, 16(6).

19  Salway, T. *et al.* "Protecting Canadian Sexual and Gender Minorities from Harmful Sexual Orientation and Gender Identity Change Efforts." A brief submitted to the Standing Committee on Health for the Committee's study of LGBTQ2 Health in Canada. Staggeringly, it was estimated in 2019 that nearly 700,000 U.S. citizens had undergone conversion therapy. See Taylor, M. C., Brown, N. T., and Conron, K. J. (2019) *Conversion Therapy and LGBT Youth.* Los Angeles, CA: Williams Institute.

20  UK Government Equalities Office (2018) National LGBT Survey: Research Report; Jones, T. W. *et al.* (2022) "Religious trauma and moral injury from LGBTQA+ conversion practices." *Social Science & Medicine*, 305.

## A brief history of conversion practices

Since the mid-1800s, homosexuality has been recognized as a distinct category of human sexuality. However, throughout the latter half of the 19th century, most doctors believed homosexuality to be abnormal and thought they could cure this "aberrant" sexuality by way of surgery[21] (early forms of the lobotomy can be traced back to the late 1800s[22]). A number of theories regarding sexual and gender variation proliferated around the turn of the 20th century, but no dominant theory emerged.[23] By the 1920s, testicle transplantation experiments, popularized by Robert Lichtenstern in Canada, were performed, where gay men were castrated and then given "heterosexual" testicles.[24] In 1952, homosexuality was listed as a mental illness in the first edition of the *Diagnostic and Statistical Manual of Mental Disorders* (*DSM*). Theories concerning sexual and gender variance continued to emerge—many of which blamed excessive parenting as the cause for such variance (e.g., an overbearing mother for male homosexuality). These theories, along with theories that attributed past sexual abuse as the cause, became medically and culturally prevalent. As of the late 1960s, behavior-modification

---

21   Streed, C. G. *et al.* (2019) "Changing medical practice, not patients—putting an end to conversion therapy." *The New England Journal of Medicine*, 381(6).

22   This information comes from a draft document prepared by Wisdom2Action, entitled "Timeline of Conversion Therapy in Canada." This document was never formally published, but I want to acknowledge where the cited information comes from.

23   Streed, C. G. *et al.* (2019) "Changing medical practice, not patients—putting an end to conversion therapy." *The New England Journal of Medicine*, 381(6).

24   This information also comes from Wisdom2Action's "Timeline of Conversion Therapy in Canada."

therapy, along with aversion therapy, was a commonplace practice to "fix" the so-called homosexual problem.[25] Some of the prominent proponents of antigay psychodynamic theories in the 1960s included Sandor Rado, Lionel Ovesey, Irving Bieber, and Charles Socarides.[26]

It was in the 1970s that the first specifically Christian ministries emerged for queer individuals seeking to become straight in the United States, though there were similar ministries in Australia that were created before their U.S. counterparts. In 1973, Love In Action (LIA) was established as the first of such U.S. ministries and would become one of the most established residential programs in the country.[27] In 1974, the Ex-Gay Intervention Team (EXIT) was started[28]. EXIT hosted the first ex-gay conference in 1976, where delegates and leaders voted to form a league of ex-gay ministries that they called Exodus,[29] which would become the largest ex-gay ministry network in the world.[30] These early ministries preached a message of change, which was only made possible through what they believed to be the trans-

25   Streed, C. G. *et al.* (2019) "Changing medical practice, not patients—putting an end to conversion therapy." *The New England Journal of Medicine*, 381(6).

26   Burack, C. (2014) *Tough Love: Sexuality, Compassion, and the Christian Right.* Albany, NY: State University of New York Press.

27   Christine M. Robinson and Sue E. Spivey, "Ungodly Genders: Deconstructing Ex-Gay Movement Discourses of `Transgenderism' in the US," *Social Sciences* 8, no. 191 (2019): 6.

28   Jim Kaspar and Michael Bussee, "A Sunday Morning Dialogue," in Issues in *Sexual Ethics*, edited by Martin Duffy (Souderton, PA: United Church People for Biblical Wellness, 1979), 143 -71; Janine Kahn, "The Closet and the Cross," *OC Weekly* (July 26, 2007), http://calstate.fullerton.edu/news/nc/072707/07-27-07_01.htm.

29   Kahn, "The Closet and the Cross."

30   Spivey and Robinson, "Genocidal Intentions," 72

formative power of Jesus. They did not draw on psychological "explanations" of homosexuality until the 1980s. However, once these ministries, along with the numerous other ex-gay organizations that later emerged, discovered supposedly scientific literature that supported their beliefs, they latched onto such teachings (even though these teachings had been increasingly disavowed by the scientific community) and incorporated them into their conversion ideology and practices. Ex-gay ministries and pseudoscientific researchers became dependent on each other—where the former received ostensible respectability by associating with those who appeared to be (but were of course not) legitimate researchers, and the latter gained followers who bought their books, resources, and programs.[31] Blending religion with this phony science, the ex-gay movement framed homosexuality as a sin, a mental illness, and a social threat—defining it as behaviors, attractions, and a "lifestyle." All this served as a way of denying both the existence and victimization of queer people. As homosexuality was seen as a condition, helping people "heal" from their so-called same-sex attractions was understood to be a compassionate and loving endeavor, rather than dehumanizing abuse.[32] These organizations, among others, were responsible for one of the most vicious, sustained attacks on LGBTQ2S+ communities in the 20th and 21st centuries.

Decades before the ex-gay movement, however, challenges to the conceptualization of homosexuality as a mental illness

---

31  Ibid.

32  Robinson, C. M. and Spivey, S. E. (2010) "Genocidal intentions: Social death and the ex-gay movement." *Genocide Studies and Prevention: An International Journal*, 5(1).

began to crop up and gained traction as time went on. Starting in 1948 with Alfred Kinsey, a number of researchers—like, for instance, Frank Beach, Clellan Ford, Evelyn Hooker, and Thomas Szasz—made clear that sexual and gender diversity is nothing less than healthy.[33] Despite this growing research, it was not until 1973 that the *DSM* declassified homosexuality as a mental illness. But in the subsequent decades, research on issues and topics related to LGBTQ2S+ communities proliferated, picking up particular speed in the late 1990s and beyond. Such research, including that which centered around conversion practices, in part helped establish queerness as a legitimate category of human identity while at the same time ameliorating the lived experiences of LGBTQ2S+ people across the globe.

This research and the many events that comprise the history of conversion therapy have given rise to numerous media representations of such damaging practices. In 2018, the films *Boy Erased* and *The Miseducation of Cameron Post* premiered, and it was these two movies, particularly the former, that significantly raised societal awareness of conversion practices.[34] This is not to say, however, that the topic was left untouched by popular media up until 2018. Indeed, in 1999, the camp classic *But I'm a Cheerleader*, starring Natasha Lyonne and featuring RuPaul Charles, premiered as the first major satirical film that pokes fun at the sham that is conversion therapy. Since then, there has been a slew of extended filmic and televisual representations

---

33   Streed, C. G. *et al.* (2019) "Changing medical practice, not patients—putting an end to conversion therapy." *The New England Journal of Medicine*, 381(6).

34   Ibid.

of conversion practices, whether they be comedies, dramas, documentaries, or otherwise. Such films include *Straight: A Conversion Comedy* (2002), *Latter Days* (2003), *Shock to the System* (2006), *Cure for Love* (2008), *This is What Love in Action Looks Like* (2011), *The Cure* (2012), *I Am Michael* (2015), *Fair Haven* (2016), *God's Law* (2018), *The Sunday Sessions* (2019), *I Am Norman* (2020), *Pray Away* (2021), *Conversion* (2022), *They/Them* (2022), and *Pedágio* (2023), among others. Additionally, though films like *Religulous* (2009) and *Brüno* (2009) do not center around conversion therapy, they nonetheless briefly treat the topic. Particular episodes of *House, Will & Grace, Our America with Lisa Ling*, and *The House of Flowers* have also focused on conversion therapy, whereas there are shorter discussions of, or passing references to, conversion practices in, for example, *Da Ali G Show, Unbreakable Kimmy Schmidt, RuPaul's Drag Race, RuPaul's Drag Race All Stars, Veep*, and *Escaping Twin Flames*. In truth, a number of these media representations are inaccurate and have made the job of activists and academics difficult as we have needed to correct the misconceptions that have arisen from them. However, these portrayals (not to mention social media discussions of conversion therapy on platforms like TikTok, Instagram, Facebook, and X) have nonetheless raised awareness of the subject.

There has, moreover, been a growing number of literary and journalistic representations of conversion therapy written by survivors. Novels and memoirs include Emily M. Danforth's *The Miseducation of Cameron Post* (2012), Anthony Venn-Brown's *A Life of Unlearning* (2014), Garrard Conley's *Boy Erased* (2016), Nick White's *How to Survive a Summer* (2017), and Peter

Gajdics' *The Inheritance of Shame* (2017). Stories by survivors have also proliferated in online publications, appearing in mainstream and queer media outlets like *TIME, Huffpost, Reuters, GQ, Queerty*, and *The Advocate*, among others. These literary and journalistic representations, in concert with those in film and television, constitute some of the artistic and investigative efforts that have shone a much-needed light on conversion practices. They are part of a growing effort to see that the long, disturbing, and devastating history of conversion therapy remains exactly that: a part of history, a thing of the past, and something that does not define anyone's present or future.

## Addressing conversion practices

In order to address and ultimately end conversion practices, it is important to identify these practices for what they are: ineffective, harmful, and dangerous. But conversion ideology and practices are more than that—they are also, as Sue E. Spivey and Christine M. Robinson have pointed out, genocidal in nature. Indeed, conversion practices target members of LGBTQ2S+ communities with the intent to completely destroy queer culture, queer identity, queer expression, and queer social vitality. Attempts to erase queer life operate on a global scale and constitute planned, coordinated, and long-term efforts. Conversion practices ought to be understood in these terms, and any resistance to ending conversion therapy needs to be identified as being complicit in these genocidal efforts. Some have argued that individuals, specifically adults, should be able to consent to such practices; however, one cannot consent to genocidal efforts, not to mention abuse and torture.[35] The only appropriate and humane way to respond to conversion practices is to do one's part in order to see an end to such efforts and support those who have gone through it.

As community, legal, and academic activists continue their fight against conversion practices, national and regional "bans" have steadily increased. Several countries have banned conversion therapy for minors; some have outlawed it in healthcare or counseling contexts; and others have criminalized any attempt to change one's sexual orientation, gender identity, or gender expression, regardless of the age of the individual or the context in which it is attempted. Some of these countries include Brazil, Taiwan, Ecuador, Malta, Germany, Chile, Canada, France, and New Zealand, whereas other countries like Spain, Australia, and the U.S. have implemented "bans" in particular municipalities or regions (e.g., certain provinces, territories, or states). However, many of these "bans" are markedly narrow and solely apply to conversion practices conducted in therapeutic contexts (e.g., in Queensland, Australia) and thus do not protect against religious conversion practices, which are, as noted above, vastly more common. Moreover, just because conversion practices have been "banned" in these national and regional contexts does not mean that such practices do not persist in many cases. Similar to all crime, when something is made illegal, it does not cease to exist; it instead goes underground. As such, we must continue

---

35 Robinson, C. M. and Spivey, S. E. (2010) "Genocidal intentions: Social death and the ex-gay movement." *Genocide Studies and Prevention: An International Journal*, 5(1).

to be vigilant in our fight against conversion therapy, no matter which country we live in.

There is a range of coded rhetoric that conversion practitioners use in order to avoid being recognized as conversion practitioners and to thus evade legal action. Such language includes not only the references to "struggling" with "same-sex attraction" but also "rapid-onset gender dysphoria"; using a "social contagion" framework in therapy; language that implies that LGBTQ2S+ identities are the result of trauma, abuse, or "grooming"; descriptions of organizations or individuals as "ex-gay"; promises, implicit or explicit, for heterosexual or cisgender identity as the preferred outcome of a counseling process; "watchful waiting" approaches to trans children; "autogynephilia" or discussions of trans selfhood as sexual-fetish behavior, not as an identity; and so on.[36] Even the language around the goal of conversion practices has changed in the last ten years, from actively promoting conversion, change, or healing to an even more deceptive goal of suppression. Of course, the goal has not actually changed, but the language used to refer to conversion practices has been diluted, so as to avoid detection by a broader public who, in the last decade or so, has become increasingly more aware of and opposed to the very idea of conversion practices than they were in the 1990s and early 2000s.[37] Spotting this sort of language is important because without knowing the dog whistles that

---

36  This information comes from another document prepared by Wisdom2Action, entitled "Service Providers Support Resource." This document was never formally published, but I want to acknowledge where the cited information comes from.

37  Csabs, C. *et al.* (2020) "SOGICE Survivor Statement, Version 4." Sydney and Melbourne: Brave, SOGICE Survivors and Brave Network.

conversion practitioners use, we cannot identify and thus stop conversion therapy from continuing to happen.

There are numerous other ways that individuals can participate in the global movement to put an end to conversion therapy. Not only can individuals and organizations report conversion practices when they become aware of them, but they can also support survivors for whom the effects of conversion therapy continue to persist. One survey indicated that the top-cited way that survivors have been able to come to terms with the effects of conversion practices was through supportive friendships with affirming individuals (regardless of their identities). Other avenues of working through the enduring effects of conversion therapy that survivors have found helpful include friendships with LGBTQ2S+ people who are out and thriving; being able to live authentically; having their emotions acknowledged and affirmed as valid; working with LGBTQ2S+ affirming therapists who address intersections of trauma, sexuality, and gender; finding and accessing safer spaces to question and deconstruct their past; and sharing their story—that is, being seen, heard, and affirmed.[38]

## Shame-Sex Attraction

This edited collection is but one of many attempts to recognize and listen to survivors. It is also an effort to address conversion practices and see to it that what happened to the contributors

---

38  Sullivan, J. *et al.* (2022) "SOGIECE/CT Survivor Support Project: Findings from a national survey, focus groups, and interviews with hundreds of survivors, 2021–22." Community-Based Research Centre.

does not happen to future generations. Contributors to this collection each believe that telling their stories constitutes powerful political praxis. By sharing what happened to them, they hope to humanize the survivors of conversion practices and to show that they are flesh-and-blood people who were subjected to dehumanizing practices that sought their erasure. They want to expose conversion practices for what they are: emphatically pseudoscientific, tragically bogus, and wildly futile means of attempting to change the sexual orientations and gender identities and expressions of countless individuals. *Shame-Sex Attraction* presents only a handful of narratives about conversion practices, as told exclusively by survivors themselves, but these stories are powerful in uncovering the various instances of conversion practices across time and space.

Contributors to *Shame-Sex Attraction* come from a variety of backgrounds and have a wide range of conversion experiences. Contributors identify somewhere along the queer sexual and gender spectrum—with lesbian, bisexual, gay, trans, and gender-queer authors included—and they variously hail from Australia, Canada, and the U.S. Most, though not all, authors come from religious backgrounds and underwent conversion therapy in religious contexts. Many of the religious narratives are written by authors from conservative Christian traditions—those who identify their former religious selves as having been a part of Catholic, white Christian fundamentalist, or evangelical traditions—but there is also one story written by a contributor who was formerly a member of a Jewish Orthodox community and one story written by a former member of what he describes as a cult. Contributors to this volume are also of various ages—

demographic information that points to the pervasiveness of conversion practices across generations.

The stories included in this collection offer a range of conversion experiences, and what unites them all is the effects of shame. Without shame, the authors in this collection would never have felt compelled to submit themselves to conversion practices. Shame is defined as the enduring negative emotion that issues forth from negative perceptions of the self, an emotion that communicates an individual's very person is defective, dirty, and offensive. Shame, as Silvan Tomkins puts it, "strikes deepest into the heart of man ... [and is] felt as a sickness of the soul which leaves man naked, defeated, alienated, and lacking in dignity."[39] Different from guilt—whose object is an actor's specific action (which does not define the actor as a person)— shame's object is the dirty, defective, and/or offensive *self*; for those who feel guilty, they know that their action was wrong, and they can move past their transgression, whereas for those who experience shame, they believe not only that their action was wrong but that *they themselves* are wrong, that their very selves are tarnished, impure, and bad. As shame is a foundational aspect of conversion therapy—and is the most cited impact of conversion practices according to one study noted above, not to mention the most common barrier to recovery[40]—it makes

---

39 Tomkins, S. (1995) "Shame-Humiliation and Contempt-Disgust." In Sedgwick, E. K. and Frank, A. (eds) *Shame and Its Sisters: A Silvan Tomkins Reader*. Durham, NC: Duke University Press.

40 Sullivan, J. *et al.* (2022) "SOGIECE/CT Survivor Support Project: Findings from a national survey, focus groups, and interviews with hundreds of survivors, 2021–22." Community-Based Research Centre.

sense why the theme of shame is explored in each of the stories compiled in *Shame-Sex Attraction*.

In addition to shame, there are a number of other themes woven throughout the stories in this collection. These include, but are certainly not limited to, hopelessness, self-hatred, depression, psychosomatic responses to conversion efforts (e.g., panic attacks, vomiting, and losing clumps of hair), damaged relationships with parents, feelings of imprisonment, shock, fear, confusion, anxiety, disassociation, paranoia, unfulfilled desire, lack of safety in religious environments, forced isolation, secrecy, a lack of authentic community, coerced activities that result in humiliation, and various other violations. As the stories in *Shame-Sex Attraction* explore these various themes, each also possesses its own tone and message. Some stories use humor, whereas others are heart-achingly serious. Some center around one moment in time, and others recount multiple events. But in every case, the negative consequences of conversion practices come into sharp focus.

In excess of how every story in this collection gives voice to the shame that is involved in and results from conversion practices, every author included in *Shame-Sex Attraction* is united by their resilience. Each author survived—and has since *thrived* despite their experience in—conversion therapy. The stories in this collection both directly and indirectly give voice to how the authors have come to terms with their pasts. That is to say, these survivors have quite literally found terms, or language, to describe their difficult and often traumatic experiences. Some offer a sense of resolution by the end of their stories, making clear how they have moved on, accepted themselves, and rejected the harmful work of conversion practices. In sharp contrast, many of the authors do not provide such narrative resolution. But this lack of resolution ought not to be read as these authors admitting defeat or expressing their resignation—their stories did not end during or after they underwent conversion therapy, and all went on to lead full and fulfilling lives in the face of their damaging experiences. I point out this lack of narrative resolution to note that its omission is intended to leave readers with the uncomfortable truths exposed by these stories. But readers will also be able to recognize how by writing their stories in their own words, the authors in this collection have the proverbial final word. Though they were once subjected to the dehumanizing work of conversion therapy, they now are the ones who control their narratives. Indeed, the very act of narrating their stories themselves emphatically underscores each contributor's resilience while powerfully speaking to each survivor's ability to move forward despite extensive hardship, scars and all.

# Chapter 1

# SNIFFING THE GAY AWAY

## GREGORY ELSASSER-CHAVEZ

"I was thinking you could use feces," she said.

"I'm sorry... feces?" I asked, for a quick second confusing the word with "Freezies," which was a term for what us college kids—with our checkered Vans and backwards baseball hats—used to call "Otter Pops."

The therapist corrected me. She did mean *feces*.

"I'm supposed to eat... feces?"

"No, no, no... you won't have to eat it; you'll just have to smell it while looking at pictures of men you find attractive."

*Oh good, that makes so much more sense.*

"For a lack of a clinical term," she continued, "you'll lust over the magazine ads depicting men you find attractive and let your mind concentrate on various sexual acts as you take several deep, diaphragmatic whiffs of the feces. You can put them in an open bowl or a Tupperware, so you can get the tip of your nose *right in* there. Do this several times until you get yourself to a point where you retch and then throw up into a toilet."

"I do this with *my* feces?" I asked, left squinting my eyes as I struggled to visually communicate the idea that the use of my own crap was the most offensive part of this entire experiment. I felt I should be offended. Was the smell of my own shit so perfectly horrendous that not one other person in the whole of humanity could come close to duplicating its rancidness?

"Um, no that probably wouldn't be a good idea. You'll want to distance yourself from the waste."

"Oh." And just before I got to questioning her about grandparents or maybe even distant cousins, she added, "Animal feces will work. You have a dog or a cat?"

"I live with my friend. At his house with his parents. They have a dog. But she's super old. Her dog's… 'patties'… have gray in them." And just as I said that, I remember weirdly thinking, and almost commenting, "They'd be *gray—g-r-A-y*, not *g-r-E-y*. Unless it were a British dog. Like the Queen's corgis."

"Doesn't make a difference," she said. Then: "Are you sexually attracted to women at all?"

"Not really. No. I mean, I find some types of painting, like, beautiful to look at, but I don't want to, like, make-out with art or anything."

"What are your percentages do you think? Compare your attraction to men versus women. 80/20? 70/30?"

To this day, I hate getting asked this question. Why the flip does this matter? Do some people automatically think that the more equal the percentage, the easier it'd be for me to swing permanently "back" to women? If it were 60% women and 40% men, would the advice be to simply give in and choose women because at least my feelings for them are above average?

I can hear it now, "You know, Gregory, a D- is at least passing…"

I don't answer this question anymore.

The therapist and her office were right out of a "1980s' Cybill Shepherd" style guide, the walls and décor splattered with pink and blue pastels, glowing under soft, halo lighting. Furniture to match. And while I was never a fashion guy, even *I* knew what straight up gaudy looked like. Turns out her office should have been draped in red flags instead of Motel 6 paintings of pink vases and neon purple ships.

This was about a month into working with her, my third or fourth therapist, and I was about ready to bail when I decided to bring up the idea of giving me homework—assignments that could include specific tasks that might contribute to the reduction of my homosexual desires. Like the time I fasted for four hours. Or that day on the beach when I prayed while pouring suntan oil on my forehead so the gay would be "anointed" out of me.

I got a zit out of that.

That was when my therapist, whose name continues to escape my memory, wondered if I had ever heard of a particular therapy called "aversion therapy," explaining that sometimes it was referred to as "conversion therapy" as it related to working with gay folks who wanted to change their sexual orientation. I hadn't, and internet searches weren't a thing yet. I couldn't do my own research. She was my only source, and she had a degree, so I trusted her.

Once she covered the basics, I told her that my brother Jim once had an elementary school teacher who went through a similar type of therapy. His fourth-grade teacher was a "bigger" gal and had gone to a clinic in order to lose weight. The clinician took a survey, making a list of favorite junk food the teacher was prone to eating that therefore sabotaged her weight loss. Doughnuts were on her list, and so they took condiments like ketchup and mustard and pickle juice, mixing them in with a fresh doughnut. They had her smell it and then eat it, so it would make her nauseous, even to the point of throwing up. This same thing was repeated every week with the doughnuts and her other favorite foods, the hope being that she would associate doughnuts, cake, and so on with repulsion and thus it would turn her off from those foods.

When I mumbled something akin to "90/10," the therapist continued. "Well, there can be two faces to conversion therapy, and we'll have you explore both. Listen, it's not enough to turn your unwanted sexual feelings into *undesirable* feelings by experiencing images and associations that are repulsive—we have to create *wanted* sexual desires by exposing you to images and associations that you will eventually find attractive."

"How... do we do that exactly?"

"Okay, let's concentrate on that 10%. What kind of women fit into those numbers?"

"You mean, what kind of women do I find attractive?"

"Yes. It's easier if you pick a couple of celebrities—that way there's little chance you'd run into them on the street, creating an unnecessarily awkward exchange."

"Um. I've always liked Kathleen Turner and Kirstie Alley."

"Hmmm. Both brunettes. Any blondes?"

"Rebecca De Mornay?" I asked, in case De Mornay wasn't

acceptable, since she, unbeknownst to a lot of people, was the daughter of Wally George, the famed, wacko American commentator, that crazy, white-haired screamer you'd have to watch on TV when an outside storm tweaked the antennae in the wrong direction and all other shows were *Poltergeist*'d out.

"Good. Get some magazine pictures of these ladies and of different men you find attractive. Cologne ads could work."

This was 1992 or '93. It was gonna take a few days, but I eventually found the photos I thought would work best.

"For the *women* photos," she said during our next session, "you get to have fun with those and as often as you'd like. But we also have to focus on the repulsion aspect, and the way repulsion is generally acquired is to consistently, even daily, introduce something to humans that produces a reaction so revolting that a person can actually vomit."

*Revolting?* I thought. Where was I going to find a church potluck on a Tuesday afternoon?

But I knew where she was going with this.

That same week, late at night when no one was around, I went into my friend's kitchen, taking a Mason jar from a cabinet that had no glass remaining because my friend and I were goofing around one day when he picked me up and slammed me backwards through the double-paned pantry door. I took the jar outside with me, located some silvery-gray-by-the-moonlight pieces, collected my specimens, and took the Mason jar back to my room. Six other people lived in that house, so I couldn't just put a jar of dog shit on a shelf inside my closet to be found by anyone who needed to borrow a t-shirt, so I grabbed my beat up Jansport backpack which was big enough to hide a notebook, a couple of good-sized books, some pens, my checkbook, some postage—yes, I carry postage with me at all times—and the Mason jar. Once organized, I put the whole thing in the closet. Pretty ingenious idea actually, putting it in a backpack, because not only would I be able to hide the crap in my bedroom, I could also take the backpack with me to do my "homework" whenever I was out of the house, since the plan was for me to do the aversion therapy a couple of times a day. It would be convenient when going to the library to work on an assignment about *The Canterbury Tales*, for example, because when the mood arose, I could duck into a bathroom stall for some special time, just me and my jar.

Turns out looking at pictures of good-looking men while taking five or six deep breaths of the dog shit throughout my day became somewhat of a challenge. It was proving difficult to do it even once a day. The end goal was to keep my nose in the jar and my eyes on the pictures—engaging in some lusting—until the retching became full-blown vomiting. Then I would be done. For that session, at least.

But I never once threw up. I couldn't make it past the retching, although I think retching is worse than vomiting. At least when you throw up you get a release—I just got a bad case of nausea that sometimes lasted a while because I could smell the shit for hours after.

Most of the time I was able to complete the task from my bedroom, but there were times I had to do it while out and about, which meant that at any given time, I was carrying a jar of dog crap. To school. To church. To get my oil changed.

Consistency was the key, but I was only able to do it for a

couple of months. Go to class, come home, look at black-and-white pictures of men advertising cologne, unscrew the lid, sniff for several minutes—that was pretty much my routine for those very long 30–60 days or so. And in order for it to be totally effective, I had to exchange the feces every few days, waiting until everyone was asleep to go outside and collect new samples.

After a few weeks, the humiliation set in. Sitting on my carpet floor with pictures propped up at various places against my closet door while holding a jar of dog poo on my lap brought about flushes to my face. Perhaps those little pinpricks on my cheeks were a response to the revulsion that was coming, or it was simply the embarrassment of knowing I was a grown man sitting crossed-legged in my room, sticking my nose in a Mason jar, inhaling dog shit.

I would no longer just pray away the gay.

I would do my best to sniff it away.

# Chapter 2

# SELF-DESTRUCTION

## D. APPLE

They say to start your story on the day everything changes.

But there was no such day.

There was only a day I unknowingly decided to destroy myself.

It sometimes takes half a Xanax, half an Imodium (always half of everything because a whole is too scary), and two cough drops to get me through this door, and I feel proud of the fact that I have taken none of those things today.

"What do you want?" the therapist repeats.

My stomach clenches immediately. I glance at the door. It would take me a mere ten seconds to run to the bathroom where I could compose myself and try again. Even if I do have an inkling of what I want, I am far too afraid to stand up and reach for it. It is selfish. There isn't time for it. What if I reach for it and they take it away, or laugh? I am not deserving.

I need permission.

I need someone to throw it at me, but I am a lousy catcher.

I don't even know what "it" is. All I know is that a piece of me is missing.

I suck in a deep, slow breath that took an entire year to learn, and grab the closest cookie from the plate she offers. My skin is on fire, and my heart races in my ears.

I blurt out the answer she'd likely been expecting: "I don't know what I want."

She settles into her high-back chair, the one that looks like a throne, but a comfy one. I have a similar chair, and if it wasn't so squishy, I'd be squirming. I poise my pen over the notepad in my lap. Funny thing, taking notes in therapy. I can never remember what we talk about after I leave, and it gives me something to do that isn't peeling back layers of my nails or crying.

She cocks her head and narrows her eyes. Usually that means somebody is trying to figure out if I am stuck up or just really screwed up. I try to hold her gaze, but my quivering lids have other ideas.

I knead the tissue on my lap. *Weak.* I nibble at the cookie. A crumb falls on the notepad, and I brush it up. "I'm really nervous right now with the way you're looking at me," I say, happy that I can verbalize anything at all.

"I'm trying to figure out what you're thinking. You have a tendency to kind of dance around issues in your head and wear yourself out before you can verbalize them."

"I guess." *Maybe that's why my family has a hard time understanding me.* I struggle for another breath without letting the floodgates open.

This is probably my fourth year speaking with her, one of countless sessions. I've gone from a crying, shaking mess to somebody who can at least string a few sentences together about themself without sobbing. My body knows what I am trying to do, and it will not let go of its armor. To my lizard brain, this is survival. I've very carefully and forcefully built my walls over the years, alternately burning in disbelief each time someone notices them.

"You've got so much talent and so much you can do. You know that, right? I really loved your short story about the ghosts."

*Aw yes, the ghost story.* I have a tendency to write my soul in fiction. It was scary to release that story into the world where people would see me. I was the mournful ghost trapped in the mirrors of a haunted hotel, cursed to travel from room to room, only where the mirrors led. All someone had to do to control me was place a mirror where they wanted or remove one. The only way to break the curse was to shatter all the mirrors and hope I survived.

I glance at the clock. A few more minutes. I know full well I will find my voice when it is time to leave and too late to talk.

I only cry in two places: one where I cannot be myself and another where I am expected to be myself. And just now I am expected to tell a truth I don't even know how to bring past my stomach. To be honest, I want nothing more than to disappear into my awkward depths.

My mother always observed that if I put my mind to something,

I would see it through, even if it was not good for me. There was nothing stopping me from self-destructing and calling it righteous.

Growing up, I was weird, wilful, quiet, had zero sense of style, and wanted desperately to understand why I was cursed to be a girl. On a scale of 1–10 for socially awkward, I was off the scale.

You see, as a conservative Christian, homeschooled family, we were used to being called weird. We embraced and celebrated the word. It didn't matter how much people outside my circle made fun of me, as long as I could retreat to safety where I was accepted.

And I was accepted as long as I walked the expected, weird path.

As a stubborn child, I had many a battle of wills with people close to me. I used to be loud about what I believed, whether it was thinking my sister got more cake than me (she'd cut her piece in half, making it look like two pieces), the name of a river (the wrong name), or that people were cheating at games (to this day I have no proof). I thought the blank days on the calendar were actually part of a month, and I refused to change my calendar to the next month. I frequently said, "Gay people are weird" (takes one to know one, I guess). Despite all my confident rantings, and people giving up on arguing with me, I had rarely felt comfortable in my own skin. All I knew was that I was damned right. It was safer, happier, more acceptable to be right—even if it wore on my parents' patience. They told me I should be a lawyer and then held on for the teenage ride.

I was constantly worried about whether or not I was enough.

I've only wanted to die two seasons in my life. The first was around the time teenage me realized I was not straight, and the second we'll get into later. How awful to be cursed with the boring and defective life of a girl *and* an attraction to the same sex... This was the wrong kind of weird. My sense of security away from the outside world faded, and I began to feel incredibly alone. Alone in a group of people, alone among family and friends. Each night, I thought the next day was an opportunity to start over and be happy, and blessed sleep would reset my life. But it was just more of the same.

I knew I wanted to die—and was quite certain God would smite me. I also knew how hell worked, and I was fairly sure anyone who was not straight went there if they gave up the ghost.

So, after writing my will, as one does at age 15, I tucked it away and thought about how to get it over with. I just hoped the smiting would happen in the night while I slept, but I kept waking up the next day.

Eventually I decided that God wasn't going to smite me just yet, and, afraid I would take matters into my own hands, I confessed all this to my mother.

My poor mother.

She is the most steadfast soul. If she had another life, she must have been a strategic planner. She could walk into a room and have it organized according to how people would use it most efficiently. She could predict stuff us kids would do. She could plan a budget, a business, a Bible study, and an entire school curriculum from start to finish. This wonderful woman never stops moving, even now. At that time, she never stopped rescuing, either.

She couldn't have known any better than to rescue me from what Christians often term *same-sex attraction*. Her life was full of religion telling her that people like me were destined for a life of destruction, sin, and separation from God. What decent, believing mother would let their child live such a life of torture?

In our family, we did everything ourselves. If for some reason we tried and couldn't, or we were in danger, we would finally ask for help. A call for help among us was serious, and we responded with the grave concern that accompanies such an ask. I knew if I asked my mother for help, she would have an answer, or she would find one with all her adult resources.

I told her about my secret: *gay, must die, going to hell*. I'd been thinking about it for years and just blurted it out, so naturally, she needed a few minutes to process this information.

I must have told her on a day she had things to do because she went out and mowed the lawn. That's something I would have done too, a task to keep my limbs busy while my brain went crazy. The women in our family accomplish our best thinking while doing something with our hands.

When she came back, I was relieved. I'd been crying, alone, and panicking. She told me how much she loved me and that she could not, would not, abandon me. It was like sitting at a doctor's office—yet another place I thought we had to be dying in order to enter.

Apparently, the answer to my predicament was that I didn't have to be gay. I could just… have God take it away. There was no need to send me off, as many kids in those days were, and worry my dad. It would be our secret.

The concept sounds silly looking back on it, but I was willing to try anything to be rid of this feeling that I was doomed and defective. I really did think being gay was a decision, and all I had to do was… un-decide. In fact, I was overjoyed to have a solution.

We read some books. We had some talks in which I had to answer if I was physically abused, masturbating, and so on. It's all kind of a blur at this point. But like any good homeschooler and self-sufficient person, I took my lessons and gathered enough information to start teaching myself.

I was my own conversion therapist.

Well, turns out when a wilful, homeschooled child does their own conversion therapy, they throw themselves into it… weirdly. For one thing, I was no adult and hadn't the life experience to be compassionate with myself.

I had nobody around to tell me just how normal it was to be gay. Heck, I thought I was possessed by the devil. I had no support group of other *not straight* kids I could see in order to know that they were not that scary or weird (weirder than me?). There were no examples of normal gay people in my life. I had no access to better information, and even if I did, I would suspect it was from Satan himself. My primary sources for all things moral were the Bible, a few chosen books, church, and some Christian teen magazines. I couldn't talk to friends or family about being gay. To be wrong, to be sinful, to be labeled as a bad person destined for hell was the worst thing I could imagine. It was a survival instinct to hide and mold myself into what would fit in. I would defend that carefully and self-righteously constructed persona as if my life depended on it.

My shining examples of people who successfully transformed were leaders of Exodus International—people who had prayed long and hard enough to marry a person of the opposite sex. They looked happy enough, and I read a few of their articles on how to change. I figured that was what I wanted, except for the married part, because guys were gross.

I prayed constantly and exclaimed my unworthiness to God every day. I held my breath and prayed for the devil to be cast out, snapped my wrist with a rubber band, bit my tongue until it bled, exhaled whenever I saw bikini ads in the newspaper and inhaled when I'd turned away. I pored over literature available to me and lingered over Bible verses threatening damnation to people I was trying not to be. I bullied myself relentlessly, all the while claiming that I didn't need love or nurturing. I could twist any thought and behavior into either God's influence or Satan's.

I could not come out of my shell, as so many people told me I should because I didn't feel as if I was inside it to begin with. But I imagined what they told me should be there, and I let people fill it. They said I was so kind when I did what they wanted; so thoughtful when I anticipated their needs; so smart when I thought like them; so strong when I rejected my heart, for it was deceitful; so quiet... well, that was one of my defects I could never shake.

And there was a resounding "No" every time I saw a beautiful woman. No curiosity. No "I like her shirt." No "hey she's sexy!"

Just "No."

*No.*

I carefully stuffed attraction to women into a box labeled "not for you" and focused on making other people happy.

Service to others kept me going. That was how I felt good

about myself. Even if the service I engaged in was performative "random acts of kindness," in public where all could see, it felt good. It was a distraction, and people were happy. I didn't need thanks. I just needed to be essential to my circle.

My need to be and be seen as a rescuer gathered momentum. The internet, and the days of message boards and chat rooms, was just taking off. I spent a ridiculous amount of time trying to convince other people to pray away the gay, like I thought I had done. I explained in detail how to do it—in fact I still remember a conversation in which I recommended this course of action to a young man who was suicidal and had asked the message boards for help. Like my mother, I was going to save him. Unlike my mother, I neglected to use proper punctuation and got obliterated by a fellow intellectual, who stood up for the person I was talking at. They were adamant that this practice had caused people to commit suicide, and it would be a very poor idea.

I had never heard of *more* depression coming from this. I had to consider, at least a little, that maybe what works for one person will not work for others. What I should have considered, was that the depression doesn't always come right away. Sometimes it takes decades.

By the time I convinced myself I was no longer attracted to women, I was no longer paying attention to Exodus International. I missed that the leaders who married opposite-sex spouses had nearly all broken down and admitted they were never cured. They were tormented every single day with being something other people wanted them to be. At their best, they divorced and sought to better themselves. At their worst, they cheated and went completely off the deep end in search of meaningful life outside themselves. It's as though they stalled at puberty and had to relearn life.

Instead of worrying about my role models fading away, I was floundering. I tried to find anywhere acceptable that I actually belonged, all the while claiming I didn't need anyone.

I had fantasies about how marriage was supposed to be. My parents told me they hadn't even kissed until they got married, which suited me fine because men were still yucky. Yet, no matter how much I tried, I only connected with guys emotionally. My first sexual experience with a man was not something I actively participated in, but once I got a taste of those feel-good cuddly chemicals, and the feeling that somebody loved me (because, you know, only people who love each other have sex), I needed that feeling.

I would do nearly anything to get it and to prevent others from feeling the absence of it.

I became severely co-dependent. I wanted to absorb everyone else's pain. I tried to rescue people and couldn't understand why they were not more grateful for my sacrifice. I took that power of learning by trial and error away from them. I eroded my interests until they meshed with those most important to me, and I told myself and everyone else that was what I wanted.

My mind started to rebel. I had no perceived control over my life, and so I found ways to make waves. I gave up friendships, stopped going to church, skipped out on family events. I even left a friend's wedding early to hang out with my boyfriend. I took my insecurities and directed them at strangers with comments about their appearance or level of straightness. My co-workers who used to enjoy being around me would hardly look at me because I couldn't tell the difference between standing up for myself and being an ass.

As my circle got smaller, my need for control got bigger. I married my on-and-off-again boyfriend. He was the first person I kissed, my best friend, and the only person who accepted me for being weird. But I didn't give him that chance to step up in other ways—I was too busy trying to fix him and avoid feeling vulnerable. I thought I could rescue him from poor spending habits, work injuries, drinking sugary beverages, expressing emotion—nearly everything I thought my family looked down on as undesirable choices. There was a time I'd even try to control what towel he used after a shower at my parents' home. After a few years, I couldn't enjoy my own hot shower, or tell what my favorite food was, because I was so obsessed with caretaking. I thought I was rescuing him from the lonely pain that I felt each day, but I was taking away his opportunities to show love and to grow, and I became bitter in the process. This was not sustainable. I couldn't grin and force myself to be happy any longer.

By the time I broke, I had no money, held three jobs, and was busy with five hobbies and trying to learn a new language just to avoid thinking about difficult, personal things. When I finally slowed down, my body hurt. My head ached. My vision blurred at random. My employer noticed a huge shift in my confidence levels. I was blacking out, and my attempts at controlling anxiety and migraines ended in many a worried look from my husband, who feared that I might start abusing anti-anxiety drugs. He needn't have worried. I was almost too anxious to take them, anyway. Having unresolved issues of his own, he did not understand the shift that was happening or how to cope with it. I began to worry that I wasn't fun enough, straight enough, kind enough, trying hard enough, for the only person who kinda got me.

I'd been to so many doctors, had so many tests and elimination diets. The one thing I never suspected, and that I used as a crutch, was the one thing that could bring me to my knees.

It was the concept that something was inherently wrong with me, that I couldn't trust my own heart or mind. This was the second time I didn't want to live, but I couldn't leave all the people I'd made rely on me.

I broke down and saw a therapist. A real one. Not just me and my self-help books, hoping that teaching myself would suffice.

✳

"Do you want to live this way forever?" The therapist cuts through my thoughts.

"What way?"

"You tell me."

I hope that's a rhetorical question because I don't have the words to acknowledge I'm unhappy. I tilt my head back and close my eyes. *Do I want to live this way forever?* My mind is blank, and all I want is for her to tell me what to do. Because I would do it for someone else. But she won't. She wants it to come from my brain. Six years ago, this kind of reflection would have sent me into a panic. Feeling anything at all would bring me back to awareness that I had a body, and that it was rebelling.

*I am safe.*

*I am safe to feel my own emotions.*

*I am lovable.*

*I can have happiness.*

Finally feeling my limbs relax into the chair, I try to gather my thoughts before saying anything. I've done the research, and I don't have to be afraid of eternal damnation. I can be me without hiding or blowing up my life. I don't need permission to live, and I don't need to draw people close, only to push them away.

I don't need to put my happiness in other people's hands, and I have no business managing theirs. *My health and happiness are my responsibility.*

*It is my right.*

*It is my job.*

The therapist is still looking at me.

"I want to live." I say the words I'd never thought I would. I had thought them often, tested them on my tongue, and decided they were not true. But this day, they are the truest words ever spoken—and they are just the beginning. "I want to be me, whatever that is, unashamed."

# Chapter 3

# BREATHLESS

### PETER NUNN

I grew up in the woods. I loved being outside and playing with my seven siblings. My happy place was the treehouse my twin brother and I had built. I would sit there and breathe in deeply and listen to the wind and life that surrounded me. I felt alive, at home, safe. I had no idea how quickly all of that could be taken from me.

When I was 15 years old, my father took me on a surprise trip. He wouldn't tell me where we were going. I had no clue what was going on, but we got on a plane in Atlanta, and it wasn't until our layover in St. Louis that he let me know that he and my mother had discovered the men's workout magazine I had hidden, and it confirmed their fear that I was attracted to men. He proceeded to tell me that he was taking me to a center to fix "whatever weird sexual shit you have going on" and that they knew that I was "same-sex attracted."

I'll never forget the drop in air pressure in the airport as he spoke. As I sat there, I struggled to keep breathing.

He continued. He told me that this was my only chance. If this didn't work, he would get rid of me; he wouldn't "have a faggot for a son." The noise and the people talking and walking and laughing around us in the airport seemed so out of place. But he pushed on as strangers walked past the two of us sitting on the end of an aisle at the gate from the plane from which we had just disembarked.

He outlined how he wanted to send me to military school to "make a *real man*" out of me but probably couldn't afford it, and he said he'd have to kick me out if not.

Finally, he stopped. He leaned back in his seat and sighed—like he'd been holding all that in and had done his part. The rest depended on me and the therapists. He could breathe. I could not.

I was quiet and submitted to him and the silence. My mind spun, and time both slowed down and sped up as we boarded our flight to Iowa. After we landed, we got a rental car and drove into Sioux City to the center I would attend for the next two weeks.

The car was a red Dodge Neon. My dad talked about how American-made cars were terrible.

We arrived at the Comfort Inn that would become my home for the next two weeks. We went into the room. My dad turned on the radio to listen to Rush Limbaugh rant about how the evil liberal mob was trying to push the gay agenda on America. My dad turned the volume up, probably to make sure I heard. I twisted the fabric of my Institute in Basic Life Principles t-shirt with my right hand while sitting on the edge of my bed. My dad called my mom and said, "We made it to the hotel," made a few grunts, and then offered a short "goodbye."

That night I stared at the popcorn ceiling. I didn't sleep at all. I cried, hoping my dad wouldn't hear. He hated it when I cried.

He told me to be a man or grow a pair. I prayed to be fixed. I thought about if I could sneak past my father's bed, get out of the hotel, and run away...

But even in my panic I knew I wouldn't leave. I knew I had nowhere to go. I had no identification, no way to fend for myself, no money. My only hope was that God would cure me of my same-sex attraction and that my family would choose to ignore my spiritual deformity and allow me to live with them.

That's where my brain was when my dad took me a few blocks away the next morning to the center. The sign on the door said, "Spiritual Warfare Center."

I waited in the butter-yellow lobby, next to a collection of fake flowers in a basket. The woman with large curled brown hair behind the sign-in desk assured my father she would keep an eye on me. She peered over her glasses and stared daggers into me. I was sure she knew why I was there.

My dad poked his head through a door and told me to follow him. I did, and we went a few doors down a hall. The room had a small couch and three folding chairs.

I sat on the couch next to my dad. I saw three items framed on the wall among the plastic potted trees. There was the famous portrait of Jesus, his soft tresses falling around his perfectly paint-ed face. There was a framed degree of the doctor whose office this was, along with a picture of the doctor standing with Bill Gothard, the founder and leader of the Institute in Basic Life Principles.

My dad stayed for only a few minutes to the best of my memory. He told me he'd see me later. I didn't know that meant in two weeks.

The doctor told me that the devil was inside me, had complete control over me, and that my very soul would be on the line in the sessions that would follow. He had gray hair that he had styled meticulously to sweep over his shining pate. His brass-rimmed glasses always seemed to sit at the end of his nose so he could look over them at me.

My childhood had shaped me to be meek, to never say no, to always obey. When I questioned, I was punished.

I didn't question anything for the next two weeks. I didn't question when the therapists asked intrusive questions about my family, my sexual urges, my body.

I didn't question them when they told me that there were no more gay people, that God had killed them all with AIDS.

I didn't question when they told me that if I didn't put in the work to "regain the ground I had surrendered to Satan," I was doomed to die alone, diseased, and unloved.

I didn't question my own faith that condemned me to an eternity in hell as a punishment for my attraction to men.

But my life after the center was even worse than those two weeks. My parents didn't talk to me about it again. I think they were perfectly happy being told it worked. I lived in constant fear of who they had told, who knew—whether or not my siblings knew about me or the pastor or friends of my parents. However, I knew.

The therapy was every bit as impactful on me as it was designed to be because it didn't end after the two weeks. I carried it home with me. I prayed and berated and loathed the queer in me. I read scripture and dove deeper and deeper into my church. But at 15 years old, my hormones were high, and sexual urges and thoughts were frequent, no matter how unwanted. My faith and the therapists at the center I attended had taught me that sexual thoughts were as much of a sin as sexual acts. Each time I was attracted to a man, I felt a little more damned, a little closer to hell, and a little more of a failure as a Christian.

Each day, I felt a little more breathless. I had told my parents the therapy had worked, and I was aware of the consequences if it didn't. I felt more and more suffocated by the terror, the desperation to be cured of this weight. I couldn't understand how if God wanted me to be straight, and if I so desperately wanted to be straight, why wasn't this working?

About a year after I left the center, I attempted suicide. It felt like my only way out. I hated myself, and I believed that God and everyone in my life did too. I wrote a note that said, "God, forgive me," and put it in my pocket. I'm so glad that I didn't go through with it—though it was not the last time I thought about it.

I spent years committing myself to the spiritual practices of prayer and repentance to try to fit into the mold of the Christian man the world wanted me to be. But that mold pulled the breath from my lungs even more. It felt like the gut punch of my dad taking me to the center all those years before that had knocked the air out of me. I felt as if I could never fully draw a full breath again. I was drowning and gasping for hope.

It wasn't until one Pride in Atlanta, years later, that I saw a sign held in the parade, hoisted high by a PFLAG mother that read, "I love my gay son," when I felt as if, maybe, I could keep going, maybe I deserved love. And maybe I could finally take a breath.

# Chapter 4

# PSYCHOLOGICAL STRIPTEASE

## CHAIM LEVIN

I still remember how cold the room seemed. As I was removing layer after layer of my clothing, it was getting colder—or at least that's how it felt. It was October of 2008, and I was alone in a locked room with my "life coach," the man who told me that if I did the recommended work, I could live out the heterosexual life that my family and community had planned for me.

I remember leaving the session and swearing to myself that I would never tell anyone about what happened in that room that day. On my way home, I remember feeling exposed as if someone had invaded my bedroom in the dead of night. I felt morbidly violated by what had just taken place. At the same time, at that point, I was still resolute in my decision to continue fighting this thing about myself that I was desperate to change: I would not accept that I was gay.

I grew up in the Orthodox Jewish community in Brooklyn, New York. I attended a school that did not teach what is commonly referred to as "secular" subjects. The school was strict, and I attended for many hours every day and was taught only religious Jewish studies, such as the Bible and Talmud. I never formally learned how to read or write in English, nor was I taught math, science, or history while in attendance.

This community was Hasidic and disconnected from the modern world. Yet, it was nonetheless a little more modern than the ones frequently depicted in TV shows and movies like Netflix's *Unorthodox* and *One of Us*. Our community thankfully did not shun the internet, and many of my peers had televisions in their homes.

As far as I knew, gay and queer people did not exist in my community. Obviously, we did, but it was only much later in my life that I understood that queer people like me were just hidden and pushed into silence. My own path deviated from that of many of the gay people in my community because unlike many others, I disclosed the secret of my sexuality during my teenage years to some friends and mentors, which is ultimately how I found myself going to my so-called life coach. I wanted nothing more than to fit into the only world I ever knew. The whispers and occasional "Fuck you, gay faggot pedophile" lobbed at me by fellow students and peers pushed me to the brink of wondering if I would ever be a full member of this community, something I desperately craved.

This is how I ended up in Alan's office attending one-on-one sessions, in addition to group sessions and a weekend retreat through Jews Offering New Alternatives to Homosexuality or JONAH, a Jewish conversion-therapy organization.

In the days leading up to this session, I had "acted out" by meeting up with someone, a man I met on the internet, and having a sexual encounter with him. I was 19, and this wasn't the first time this had happened, but as with almost every previous encounter, this one took place in the dead of night while my brain was in overdrive and my body was physically exhausted. I was grappling with extreme feelings of guilt and was worried that I was at risk of catching all kinds of diseases given my limited— or non-existent—knowledge about safe sexual practices. This was how these situations unfolded at the time: I would spend long hours or even days searching online for sexual encounters with other men. While doing these searches, I fooled myself into thinking that I wasn't actually planning on meeting someone; I was just browsing. And then, when the moment arrived, often at ridiculous hours like 3 am, I would finally connect with a fellow closeted man from my community, and he and I would do the deed.

I arrived at Alan's office the day after this latest encounter, feeling small and as if I wanted to hide from myself. I couldn't believe it had happened again. Here I was, 18 months into this program, still having sex with men. How could it be? Why wasn't it working? Why was I doing this? Why did it feel that with every passing day these desires for men got more intense and my ability to control them only weakened?

These feelings were only exacerbated by the fact that the morning after this encounter my then-best friend and co-worker came over and opened my computer and saw my entire chat with the person from the night before. I was stupid enough not to close out all the tabs and hide my tracks. "I saw the whole thing," he said. "It's so disgusting. I can't believe you did that—honestly, so gross."

I was in the perfect state of mind for Alan to do to me what he did to so many other clients before and after I went to his office. I was in a particularly vulnerable state of mind, and that was usually when Alan made his move. Alan himself was someone who in his own words "struggled with same-sex attraction." Later, in court, the founders of JONAH would describe Alan as a "heterosexual with a homosexual problem." Like many people who worked in this field at the time, he became a life coach and started "counseling" people, despite not having any formal counseling degree or credentials.

Somehow our discussion became about my feelings of inadequacy and about my manhood, a common theme in the conversion-therapy universe and a trope that is often used to explain reasons why men are gay: a masculinity deficit. Alan "invited" me to stand in front of a mirror while holding a large wooden staff with my right hand. I had heard vague references about people taking their clothes off in front of him, but I didn't think much of it because I never believed it would happen to me—or rather, I never believed I would allow it to happen to me. Alan instructed me to find negative messages about myself and say them out loud. He then told me that when I was "ready," I should remove a layer of clothing that corresponds to these negative messages.

"I am weak"—take off my shirt.

"I am needy"—remove my shoes.

"I am vulnerable"—no more pants.

These are some of the messages that I repeated out loud, curated with the "help" of Alan, and that were then used to manipulate me into removing my clothing. I distinctly remember feeling and registering a strong objection to continuing this exercise, but one of the fundamental and most manipulative aspects of this "therapy" was that whenever I felt an objection to something it was used against me to "challenge" me to overcome something I was afraid of. The implication relied on ideas of exposure therapy, where if I resisted something, that meant I had to engage with it. If I feared it, I had to do it in order to overcome that fear.

"I don't feel comfortable taking off these layers," I said.

"What do you think is going on for you that is causing you to feel this discomfort? It sounds like something you need to work through in order to get to where you want to be," replied Alan.

"I am not comfortable being this exposed," I said.

"But this is part of the work that you need to do in order to conquer your same-sex attraction," was his reply.

The implication was that if I did not succeed at ridding myself of my gayness by taking off my clothes—or doing anything else he told me—it would be my fault and not the fault of the program.

And so there I was, standing completely naked, in front of a mirror, holding a tall wooden staff with Alan sitting a few feet to my right on a black stool that had no back. It was in that moment that he once again "invited" me to touch myself in the place where I felt my masculinity. He did not say that I should touch my penis, at least not outright. He asked me, "Where do you feel your masculinity lives?"

I responded questioningly, "My penis?"

Alan invited me to "hold" this masculine part of myself. I again resisted this invitation, but he again reminded me that this was part of the work that I needed to do, so I relented and followed his instruction. As I grabbed myself, I let my mind go blank, free of any thought, free of what was happening.

My main goal was to end this humiliating moment as quickly as possible.

Once Alan was satisfied with my "work," I was invited to put my clothes back on piece by piece.

"I am beautiful, hot even"—I put my underwear back on.

"I am powerful"—I put my undershirt back on.

"I am strong"—I put my shirt back on.

"I am capable"—I put my pants back on.

"I am worth it"—I put my socks back on.

"I matter"—I put my shoes back on.

This only took five minutes compared to the 30 minutes it took to reach this point. Without realizing it at the time, this session would change the trajectory of my life forever.

Chapter 5

# THE RAGE TO LIVE

## JORDAN SULLIVAN

I should have been born with a penis.

I knew that from when I was 4 years old. As a 10-year-old, I began to pray for God to give me this one thing I knew would prove that I was a boy and not a girl.

*With God, all things are possible.*

If I just had enough faith, it would happen. Every morning I lifted my bed covers, hoping my prayers had been answered, and every morning I would cry, believing I didn't have enough faith.

One morning, overcome with guilt for masturbating to fantasies about girls, I crept downstairs before my mother was up. I found a sharp cutting knife and placed my right hand on the counter. I lifted the knife with my left hand, holding it over my right index finger (the *offending* finger). I prayed for the courage to cut off the part of my body that "caused me to offend," but I couldn't do it. I was overcome with guilt for not having the courage to do what I perceived as God's command. *If your right hand causes you to sin, cut it off and throw it away.*

A few months later, shortly after my 11th birthday, my faith and my sexuality were about to collide head on. On a Sabbath morning in 1971, I was slowly roused from sleep, disturbed to recall the dream out of which I had awoken. In it, I had been a man making love to a woman. I was overcome with guilt as I realized that I was wet "down there."

It was the day of my baptism. To awaken with such sinful thoughts and desires on the morning of such a special day horrified me and reminded me just how unclean and sick I was. How could I take part in such an act while being so completely unclean?

Overwhelmed with guilt and shame, I attended church, was baptized, and gave my heart and soul to the God I loved. I walked into the change room immediately afterwards, where I dried off and dressed. My mother had placed a pair of clean underwear in a bag, and as I pulled them on, my eyes welled up with tears. I closed my eyes and bowed my head in shame when the clean white material touched the unclean, shameful part of my body. The fear and guilt around my sexuality, and its conflict with all I held to be true and pure, were intensifying.

I read my Bible as a young child, and at age nine, I began reading books by Ellen G. White, considered a prophet by Seventh-day Adventists or SDAs. I absorbed the belief that I was an abomination in the sight of God, sexually perverted, that masturbation would lead to insanity or an early death, and that I was in danger of being lost for eternity. My prayer life increased and I constantly memorized scripture to keep "demonic harassment" at bay.

In *Messages to Young People*, White instructs believers:

Go to your closet, and there alone plead with God: "Create in me a clean heart, O God; and renew a right spirit within me." Be in earnest, be sincere… Agonize. Jesus in the garden sweat great drops of blood; you must make an effort.

But no matter how hard I tried, I was unable to stop the sinful thoughts and feelings.

Fast forward 16 years, when I was a schoolteacher in the beautiful foothills of the Sierra Nevada mountains in northern California. I taught all eight grades in a one-room schoolhouse for faculty children at the Weimar Institute, at the time an unaccredited boarding academy and college—from which I had graduated—and a health institute, created by a small group of very conservative Seventh-day Adventists.

On a beautiful sunny day late in January, I met up for lunch with my best friend Leslie. Afterwards, she passed me a booklet.

"I'd like you to read this," she said.

I glanced down and read, *Emotional Dependency: A Threat to Close Friendships*, published by Love In Action, a Christian change ministry based in southern California. I quickly thumbed through it and discovered to my horror that it was written for lesbians. My friend said, "Read it for the emotional part, not the physical." She also said something about needing some distance between us for the next while, but I didn't really process it. I was already in shock. I had never acted on my attractions, never talked about them at all, so how could she know? I muttered a quick thank you and headed back to work.

While my students worked in the library, I read through the booklet which seemed to describe me perfectly. I was thrilled because it seemed to offer an explanation of my "problem," but I was also horrified. Although I had never acted on my "homosexual tendencies," I could no longer deny what was now staring me in the face.

The next day I was barely able to function. I spoke with the campus chaplain about "emotional dependency," and he recommended a book, *The Road Less Travelled* by Scott Peck, which argues that dependency "is pathological—it is sick, always a manifestation of a mental illness or defect." This seemed to confirm the fears I had carried since childhood—that I would end up in a psychiatric institute.

For the next three months I continued to teach, while deeply depressed, anxious, angry at Leslie for abandoning me, and overcome with an increasing sense of hopelessness.

On a sunny spring morning in 1987, I came to the conclusion that the only option left for me was suicide. I had spent my life holding things together for God, church, parents, friends, and my career, but all seemed to have failed me. None of them provided sufficient reason to live. *I* was the one who had to live with this pain, not them, and it just wasn't worth it anymore. I scribbled the following on a pad of paper:

> Today I wonder if I might be lucky enough to have the courage to give myself "hope." Hope that I won't have to bear this long, that someday soon I can make sure that the pain, suffering, agony, sickness, and guilt will be over. There is no reason to continue. No reason to go on like this. So why go on? The word itself seems wrong to write, but it has become a logical, almost accepted part of me. Suicide. The loss of the will to live. The utter despair. The giving up of hope.

So many years I've hidden and shrank away,
Until finally the secrecy has become my greatest enemy.
I tire of life and its endless problems, seemingly unsolvable.
Caring no longer, I yearn for the ending of it all.
In hopeless agony I push away all "friends," too afraid to
share,
Determined not to let them see me hurting, confused and
weak.
Every path is strewn with hopelessness.

... **SUICIDE** – the only answer.

My prayer became *I am incapable of comprehending, blind to the truth, scarred by sin. My nervous system feels shot. I can't hear you anymore. I can't see you anymore. I've caved in from within, and there's no one or nothing to reach inside and put the shattered pieces back together. Your avenues to my soul are shattered. I'm a shell, with nothing – no one...*

I'll never forget the quiet, detached way I made the decision to end my life.

I actually felt a rush of joy, knowing the self-loathing, depression, loneliness, exhaustion of suppressing my energy and emotions, and the constant fear of being discovered for what I was, would soon be over. The next day I went into town and unexpectedly bumped into Leslie. The shock of seeing her, while planning my own suicide, shook me up enough to realize I needed help. But I couldn't talk to her.

There was only one person I could think of to whom I might

dare to speak the truth: Bev, a faculty member at the college and also the mother of a close college friend. The next morning, I knocked on her door, and for the very first time in my life, I spoke the words "lesbian" and "homosexual" out loud, expressing my fear that I was one. At the same time, I shared my plan to commit suicide.

There was no surprise from Bev, no rejection, no horror in reaction to my announcement, just a calm, loving, concerned friend. She provided a safe place to talk while making us both a delicious strawberry smoothie, which we took with us on a walk outside. Her ability to listen without judgment and her acts of kindness provided me with the courage needed to start the long uphill climb of facing and dealing with my "homosexual tendencies."

The last three months had taken a great toll on my health. One afternoon in early May, I decided to go for a hike among the rolling hills. As I ascended one particularly steep hill I was stopped by a sharp pain in my chest. Gasping and clutching my chest, unable to breathe, I sat down on the hillside expecting to die right then and there. But the pain and breathlessness slowly subsided.

Once I was able to stand, I made my way to Bev's home. I opened the door and collapsed on the floor. She immediately took me to a doctor who told me that I was experiencing panic attacks and needed to leave immediately to care for my health. I resigned from my teaching position and took a bus to Portland, Oregon, where a cousin agreed to let me stay for some much-needed rest and recuperation.

Three weeks later, I returned to California to pack my belongings and flew home to my parents, just east of Toronto. I didn't know where else to go. I announced my anger and bitterness toward my friendships, the Weimar Institute, Ellen White, the Seventh-day Adventist church, and God, believing they had all failed me when I needed them most. My parents provided me with a safe space during those dark days, without asking questions and allowing me to just be.

Even though my faith had been shattered and I no longer attended church, conservative Christianity was the only world I trusted. I absorbed everything I could: books, cassette tapes, and newsletters, from places such as Love In Action and Exodus International. I counseled with an SDA pastor for a short time who referred me to an SDA Christian counselor.

At one particularly challenging session with him, I learned that my "homosexual tendencies" were a result of childhood traumas and an unhealthy relationship with my mother. I arrived home, filled with rage and agony. All the pain and self-loathing, all the agony I had lived through since I was a child was because of my mother?! She was the reason for my attractions to girls? She was the reason I felt more like a boy than a girl? She was the reason for always wanting to die? I opened my mouth in a silent scream of rage and betrayal as I fell to my knees, tears streaming down my face.

I never questioned what I had been told, and even as an adult I was not yet able to question what my counselor was telling me. I had been raised in a very closed religious community, where nothing outside our faith was trusted.

I continued to work desperately to become heterosexual. Instead of being "healed" or changed, I gained over 150 pounds, distancing myself even further from my body. As a young teenager, I had consciously worked at "not moving" in order to silence the masculine energy in my physical body. Those efforts now included stuffing down my fears and emotions through overeating.

By the end of my first three months in counseling, I was physically and emotionally drained. Fortunately, my vacation plans had been timed perfectly, and I flew out to San Francisco to visit friends and be a bridesmaid in my friend Tonia's wedding. I was determined to play the part, even if it included putting on a costume and pretending to be someone I wasn't.

After the reception had started, I retreated to the bathroom for a silent cry. I was no longer able to keep up the pretense. I spoke briefly with Tonia who found a car for me to drive back to her parents' house where I was staying. When I arrived, I immediately ripped off the dress, nylons, and high heels, and jumped in the shower where I ended up screaming and sobbing as I literally rubbed my skin raw—desperate to remove the makeup and hating my body and the pretense of presenting as a woman.

Over the next few months, I pulled further away from my parents, especially from my mother, believing my struggle with homosexuality was due to her mistakes. It was difficult. Therapy did lead to some learnings that helped me have a healthier relationship with my parents. But, along with that, explanations for my "learned perversion" were constructed in an attempt to explain away my homosexuality.

After years of this intense self-analysing, I found myself once again attracted to a woman. I was devastated. In fact, the homosexual desires seemed even stronger. At last, it dawned on me that denial and suppression of one's desires was not change.

In 1993, I entered into a year of study, reading everything I could find on scripture and homosexuality. *For the first time in my life,* I was open to reading theological arguments on the "other side of the issue." But as convincing as the arguments were for accepting my sexual orientation, I wasn't able to do it.

One night, after spending the entire night in prayer, I lay face down on the floor, exhausted from wrestling with God's silence. And suddenly in that silence, I heard a quiet, calm, but very clear voice, "I have no problem with you being a lesbian. You're the one who can't accept it."

At that moment, I realized just how much my personal fears, judgments, assumptions, and prejudices about what it meant *to be homosexual* got in the way of being able to hear what God said or didn't say, and in the way of embracing my sexuality.

At last, I was able to accept myself and came out as a lesbian at the age of 33.

In my 40s, I decided to address why I couldn't seem to care for my physical body and health. It took seven years of therapy, much of it energy and body-based work with an LGBTQ2S+ affirming therapist, before I realized that my physical energy was much more masculine than feminine.

When my therapist asked if I thought I might be transgender, I blurted out, "NO!" in disgust. That night I wrote in my journal, "No! I do not want to transition to be a man! But oh, how I'd love to have a strong bare chest with muscles and no female breasts. Oh, how I would still love to have a penis. No contradiction there... Duh!"

One day in 2007, my parents called to tell me they had just watched an Oprah Winfrey episode, "Born in the Wrong Body." "I think I finally understand you!" my father said excitedly. I remember being disgusted and shutting him down politely. When I worked up the courage to watch the show, it was eye-opening. For the first time, I heard a female-to-male trans person tell their story—and it was *my* story! That night I wrote in my journal, "I feel like I've just been handed back the missing part of myself..."

During that fall, I came out to my family, who had totally affirmed me as a lesbian, with the truth of what I was realizing— that I identified as gender queer. At the same time, my mother was dying of cancer, and after her death on January 2, 2008, I shut down for over a year.

I was working at the national office of The United Church of Canada at the time, and in late 2009, I was asked to work with the Trans and Gender Diversity Task Group where I met with people of diverse gender identities. I learned a lot from listening to their experiences. Cindy Bourgeois, the first openly trans woman ordained in the United Church, encouraged me to attend a "Gender Journeys" support group at Sherbourne Health in Toronto. It was there, in 2011, that I was able to connect with trans men, discover books by trans men, and meet a therapist who was a trans man, who later became my therapist. I was able to continue my journey toward full acceptance of my body's masculine energy and gender identity.

At the age of 51, with the full support of my father, sisters, friends, and colleagues, I announced that I was going to transition. While I have lived as a trans man for over 12 years now,

I am still learning that when you suppress a part of your core identity—you dissociate from yourself—and it can take years to re-integrate and become whole.

I continue to *rage to live* and work to end the practices that harm and traumatize people's core identities and to support survivors like myself.

As queer and trans people, all we ask is to be loved and valued for who and what we are.

# Chapter 6

# AWAY AND AWAY

## NATHAN XIE

I wrote an autofiction novel because I believe to make art is to make new meaning. I wanted to make art out of the ugly things in my life. Otherwise, they were just luggage going around and around the baggage carousel of my mind. I wrote about being raised in the cult my mother believed in: Falun Dafa. I wrote about being coerced into the heart of the cult: the Mountain. I wrote about playing the cello for the Master's performing arts group: Shen Yun. I wrote about eight years of hiding my queerness in accordance with the Master's teachings on transcending into godhood. I wrote about leaving the Mountain, Shen Yun's headquarters and training compound in Cuddebackville, New York, after graduating from its somehow-state-accredited college at age 22. I wrote about my first date with a man who was the fictional version of my real-life boyfriend. I wrote about how my disappointed parents spied on my every move, discovered my date with the man, and then kicked me out of the house.

Here the narrative diverges.

I didn't write about my three days of homelessness and how my boyfriend, at the time a man who I had gone on only a single date with, couldn't help me—he wanted to, but he didn't have the resources to provide refuge, and nobody else he knew did either. I didn't write about how I begged my parents to let me return home and how they relented under the condition that I turn straight.

I didn't write about my mother commanding me to read and reread aloud with her the Master's holy book *Zhuan Falun*, his various lectures, and his condemnations of homosexuality month after month.

I did write down where the condemnation came from: Teachings at the Conference in Switzerland, 1998, in which the Master declared homosexuality a violation of the standards gods set for mankind, how they designed a slow annihilation exclusively for people like me. Starting from the skin, the gods peel away thinly cut layers of queer flesh, over and over again to maximize the pain until death truly is a mercy.

I didn't write about my mother's knee grazing against mine while we read the Master's lectures, no warmth passing through the fabric of our trousers, the hardwood floor pressing through a thin carpet against the bones of my ass as I sat for hours, the Master's principle of Tolerance reverberating through me. I didn't write down my mother repeating the Master's last words in his condemnation at regular intervals: "A person should live in an upright manner, living honorably like a human being. He shouldn't indulge his demon-nature and do whatever he likes." I didn't write down my mother forcing me to look her in the eyes as she quoted the Master. I didn't write down her asking me: "Do you understand?" I didn't write down her asking me: "Do you truly understand?"

I didn't write down the feeling of telling her lie after untruth after evasion after apology between the Master's lectures, how my lips and the words they spoke estranged themselves from the rest of my body, how perhaps it was vice versa, how vividly and clearly I saw the son my mother wanted: a man who never gave up Falun Dafa, who happily read about massacring queer people with his mother, and the only man he ever loved, the Master.

I did write about how this belief of death to all queer people united my mother and father, even though he despised her Master; if I couldn't transform into a straight man, my father would hold my mother's hands before the carpaccio slices of my corpse, and he would tell her, "Don't cry. He deserved it."

I didn't write about my father sitting me down at the kitchen table and placing a contract he created before me—the terms: my parents confiscating my phone every night, them choosing my graduate school major, them permitting me to apply to only one college, every class to be completed online and within my parents' house, and on my graduation and finding work, all my income would go into a bank account they controlled until I married a woman they approved of. I didn't write down my frustrated response or my father's reply: "I'm not stupid enough to trust you with any freedom or resources independent of me. If I catch even a whiff of another man, I won't hesitate to throw you out on the streets again."

I didn't write down that after I was accepted into the one program I was allowed to apply to, I asked permission to borrow the car to visit a friend who was still on the Mountain, and after I returned, my father accused me of meeting a man, specifically my boyfriend. I didn't write about watching through a wall of frosted glass my incoherence, my hand-wringing, my exclamations to make a point with volume in lieu of sense. I didn't write down my father's call to my friend, who miraculously covered for me.

I didn't write about how I maintained a long-distance relationship with the man who became my boyfriend during the months I spent imprisoned in my parents' house, about the old phone I hid from my parents, or about my boyfriend's sexting, how through his words I returned to my body, then left my body as soon as I came into my hands. I didn't write about seeing my boyfriend for the first time many months after the first date had gone wrong, how hard it was to stay in my body as we walked around a frozen lake, as we laid under the off-white blankets in a cheap and chilly hotel room, as I fielded calls from my father and mother every other hour. I didn't write about saying, "I love you," to my boyfriend for the first time, how I didn't trust my words, didn't trust myself to love anyone. I didn't write about leaving my boyfriend at 6 pm, feeling not only sadness for the briefness of our date, but also a bitter relief.

I didn't write about making dumplings from scratch with my mother, about kneading the dough, slicing it into small pieces, rolling them flat and round and perfect, then handing them to my mother to stuff and close, or about eating the dumplings as my mother described my future wife. She was Chinese, she believed in Falun Dafa, and she was a better person than me. I didn't write about imagining how lovely the dream wedding with my future wife was, my parents smiling and crying and enjoying themselves, finally free from any obligation to manage my waywardness, and then the sweet child my future wife birthed, a child I didn't raise the way my parents raised me, and that the child didn't come from sex since my future wife consented to never sleeping with me; instead, I went to a sperm bank and masturbated to men in my head, the only place men could be naked before me. I didn't write down the profound joy of appeasing my parents, overwhelming any of my other unfulfilled desires, and how natural it felt to continue resisting my body, my mind, myself because I had done so all my life, to use the Chinese character of Tolerance as a mantra: 忍, 忍, 忍. I didn't write about how much pain I could tolerate and by which I could be redeemed, how much less pain I would need to tolerate if I didn't abandon my parents and their values. I didn't write down that my future wife looked like a younger version of my mother. I didn't write about how much I loved her. I didn't write about how much I despised her. I didn't write about how much I pitied her. I didn't write down how often I asked myself, *What did she do to deserve so much suffering?*

I didn't write about the evening my father offered me a glass of vodka after dinner and the career and salaries he overestimated for me, which I would use to support his and my mother's retirement, since they couldn't afford one; he made so many leaps of faith even though the only master he believed in was money. I didn't write down how close I came to converting to my father's faith instead of my mother's, since my grandfather from his side was paying for my graduate studies; I agreed to turn straight not only because my boyfriend couldn't save me but also because of my grandfather. I didn't write down how regularly my father insisted I talk to my grandfather, who spoke a dialect I couldn't understand, who told me a pretty girl recently moved in next door to him, and I promised, at my father's prompting, to visit my grandfather and his neighbor as soon as I could. I didn't write down my father telling me my grandfather was on the brink of death, how my grandfather needed to see me marry a nice woman and pass the family name down to the next generation and that I better live up to the sacrifices every man before me in the family had made. I didn't write down how my father's voice broke as he told me this. I didn't write about how my father invented and hyperbolized achievements of mine to my grandfather on hours-long phone calls. I didn't write about how proud I felt hearing my father's pride in a son he didn't have.

I didn't write down my mother's reasonable demand that I contribute to the household chores, vacuuming and washing the dishes, then my mother's reasonable complaints that I kept missing spots. I didn't write down how she observed I was missing something critical, but so was she. Her reasonable complaints became screams, became cries, became verbal beatdowns, she couldn't articulate the one flaw she most wanted to see resolved, but there was no evidence I could provide of turning straight. I didn't write about the hours I spent locked away in my room so my mother couldn't yell into my ear as I waited for my father to return home and calm her down, but when he returned, he listened to my pleas with indifference and said: "She's your mother. You have to endure this."

I didn't write about how every time I took a shower, clumps of hair fell out. I didn't write about the morning all the flesh in my upper back ossified and whenever I tried to break the stone encasing, mind-shattering pain shot through my neck and exploded behind my forehead. I didn't write about my attempt to break up with my boyfriend. I didn't write down how right my father was—I must endure this.

I didn't write about how much more I could endure, or tolerate, or disassociate from, depending on which part of me was interpreting the event impacting me. I didn't write down how I actually left my parents. It was three months before I graduated from my program, my parents both left for work one day, I packed what few belongings I wanted to take with me, my boyfriend picked me up, I left behind a brief, meaningless letter for my parents, and then I holed up in an apartment I paid for with a student loan I had secretly applied for and placed in a bank account I had secretly created. I didn't write down how I saw my departure as an elevation of endurance, of tolerance, and of the estrangement I experienced with myself. I was long gone the moment I agreed to convert into a straight man for my parents, and still I needed to blast myself even further away.

Now I have returned. I can think through the decisions I made or didn't make or couldn't make.

I didn't write down what I didn't write down then because I couldn't imagine it as art. So often a recounting of suffering is too crippled by itself to be anything more than what it is—someone telling you it hurts here, here, and here, and they don't know why these wounds appeared, only that the human body is a vulnerable and sensitive and mysterious and maybe even beautiful thing asking the world when the bleeding will stop. Without new meaning to make out of this experience, writing it down would be purely emotional gratification. Not for myself—rather, for the sadistic stranger who wants to enjoy a plate of medium-rare pain.

My first experience of creating art was reinterpreting and

redefining and rewriting my autofiction novel time and time again from as many angles as necessary. I could only do this with the distance of knowing my novel is a work of art separate from myself. It transcends me. This piece I have written here is different. I processed what happened to me and how I felt, and I have enlightened to nothing but an observation of what is. I'm not sure this can be called art.

# Chapter 7

# THE SCRIPT WE'RE GIVEN

## LEXIE BEAN

I am bringing you back to this room. Yes, one that had a shared couch that is navy and dented. A barred lamp equally IKEA in aesthetic—angular and accidentally cold. It could be a room that you would know—beige walls and cornered with toys for a cat that's not my own.

Sit down by my side because the show is about to start. I pull my phone out of my pocket, not quite prepared for its harsh light.

I draw my feet in closer to say, "This is what happened before *it* happened—the attempt to help me find my 'true self.'" I tell it to you in a script because maybe I want to pretend that it wasn't us who said this, who did this. Maybe a script is my way of offering forgiveness through distance or safety through an imaginary witness we all needed. It's as if to say that something much larger than us wrote the lines for her. Are you her? I am not sure. If you are, I wish to add: "I don't want to hold us hostage to time nor memory." I wish to add: "I know you're not the only mother-figure who has been scared." It's not about haste, or blame, but the acknowledgment that the desire to convert someone comes from the wish to be in the same world.

So, here is the script I offer, with uncertainty that either of us knew how to do it any differently.

### Living room, early afternoon

We see Lou hesitantly sitting down on the couch. Lou struggles to find another way to put off this phone call, instigated by a text from Mom that reads, "Please call me."

After a few moments of holding a pillow, Lou presses the "call back" button, knowing exactly what this call is going to be about. They both try to enter it with confidence.

LOU:     Hello?

CAROL:  What are you up to?

LOU:     I was just eating lunch and then talked with Deb for a while. Um, she leaves for Argentina tomorrow.

CAROL:  Who?

LOU:     Deb. She's leaving for Argentina tomorrow.

CAROL:  What's she doing? I can't hear you.

Mom is becoming increasingly scattered in her thoughts. It is clear this is not what she wants to be talking about.

LOU:    She's going to Argentina tomorrow.

CAROL:  Oh, I see. That's nice.

LOU:    So, what's going on? Is there an emergency?

CAROL:  You know, I don't go on Facebook very often. And today when I was scrolling, I saw this article... thing.

Mom begins a monologue that she has given to Lou many times before.

CAROL:  I have done everything for you. I'm your biggest fan. Why didn't you talk to...

LOU:    Can I...

CAROL:  I *just don't* understand why you don't talk to me. Why would you post it on some... some website before even telling me? You know you can tell me anything. I love you. (beat) You were literally just home, and now I see this thing. I am your mother, Louise. I know you better than anyone else. And I've watched you your entire life and there is nothing boy, nothing masculine about you. You have grown into a beautiful...

LOU:    Can I speak for a minute?

Lou takes a moment to gather thoughts and stay in control.

LOU:    I'm sorry it happened this way. It wasn't my plan. I was going to tell you in a few weeks when I felt ready.

84

(beat) Plus, I don't even want to be a man. Did you read what I wrote? I am both. I am somewhere in between. I'm just trying to live honestly and let every part of me survive.

CAROL: I didn't read it... I just... Look, you don't have to go on changing like this. You can be whatever you want—gay, lesbian, whatever. I have let you wear whatever you want, cut your hair any way you want. But a surgery... What is that all about?! What's wrong with your *beautiful* body? I love you the way you are.

LOU: I know that you love me and there's nothing wrong with my body. It just feels like something between me and the world.

Lou hesitates to explain the surgery knowing that it won't go well.

LOU: (long pause) It's called top surgery. It's basically getting breasts removed.

CAROL: What?! Oh my god, you want to *cut off* your breasts?! Oh, I am very concerned, Lou. What's wrong with your breasts? Dammit, I love you, and there are so many people who love you too. You can't...

Lou's patience begins to run short.

LOU: People love me because I am changing, and they choose to love me every step of the way.

CAROL: This is so drastic. Surgery is so drastic. You need to see a professional. Someone who can help you know what you really want. You need more time to think about this.

Mom speaks with fear, as if she can feel Lou slipping away.

LOU: I live in my body. This may seem drastic for anyone not living in my body, but I know what I need. It seems like you're the one that needs to go to therapy.

Lou has a brief moment of feeling empowered.

LOU: I talk with people about this all the time. I'm so grateful to have people in my life who let me be honest. This is new for you, and that can make it feel scary. You're letting what you don't know make you afraid. (long pause) Yeah.

CAROL: No, you need to talk to someone one-on-one. You're too young to know about regret. (long pause) So, you want to just cut off your breasts?

LOU: Technically yeah... but there is a lot more to it.

CAROL: How can there be more to it?

LOU: It's not about cutting myself up or off. It's about becoming closer to how I really feel. Like... when I walk into a room, people only see me as a woman and that's not who I am. A big part of me is lost in every interaction I have and… I'm tired.

CAROL: Oh, I don't think they do. I haven't seen any of that.

Lou feels the sting of denial.

LOU: You don't live in my body! Even the last time I was home, and I laughed when I saw an old picture of me on the mantle, and I said, "Oh, that doesn't look like me." And you said, "Yes it does." And then I was like, "No, it doesn't." (beat) I need you to believe me.

CAROL: I do believe you. Don't put words in my mouth.

LOU: Therapy can't fix me the way you want it to!

CAROL: I'm not trying to fix you. It's just that surgery is so dangerous. You can just get a haircut or…

LOU: But we can't be afraid of change. I know that you love me, but that doesn't mean you can't love whoever I become and who I am and what I move toward. I am ongoing. I'm going to spend the rest of my life changing. I know what's best for my body, and I know that this surgery will give me something important. It will help me feel more like myself. I haven't been myself in so many years, so many parts I have shut off. I honestly mourn those lost years.

CAROL: Really? You weren't yourself in college either?

LOU:     Not really. I still limited myself a lot and of course received influence all the time from TV, or, I don't know, every time I walk into a new place and notice how people choose to interact with me. A lot tells me who I am and what I'm capable of. I don't know.

CAROL:   Hm. I've never experienced that before.

LOU:     You don't think you're affected every time someone talks to you or every time you turn on the TV? We get this stuff all the time, and it makes it hard to believe in options. (beat) For example, the things you're saying to me are affecting me right now.

CAROL:   And you're affecting me right now too... What does this have to do with cutting off your breasts? I can't believe you don't love yourself enough to get surgery. I love your body.

LOU:     Well, I don't!

CAROL:   You don't? You see this is why you should get therapy...

LOU:     Well, I do, but I just don't love the way it fits into this world or my spirit. It's my body, and I have the right to do what's best for it. This is my decision. (beat) Just like you know what's best for your body. (long pause)

CAROL:   I don't always know what's best for my body. (long pause)

The conversation is going nowhere.

LOU:     Well, you still have the right to make choices. (long pause) I think I need to take a break from this conversation.

CAROL:   I just need to say something. I know it's going to make you upset, but I have to say it. (long pause) For the past ten years or so... I've noticed that you're easily influenced by the people you hang out with.

LOU:     What do you mean?

This hits Lou harder than any other point in the phone call.

CAROL:   I told you not to get upset. You always do this.

LOU:     The people who make me feel safe are a bad influence? I share myself with the people I do because I see myself in them. They make me feel brave, and they make me feel as if I have options in this world.

CAROL:   Who makes you feel like you don't have options?

LOU:     Almost everyone!

CAROL:   I'm very worried about you. I know how impulsive you can be... cutting up your beautiful body. I am your mother. You are a part of me, and I am responsible for your happiness. You don't need to talk with your friends; you need to talk with a professional.

LOU: Okay. I'll think about it... but here's the thing: I'm excited to get this surgery. It doesn't have to be this tragic thing. I'm excited to be closer to how I feel, and I'm grateful to have so many people supporting me along the way.

Mom doesn't know what to say and begins to tear up. Her sadness builds until the end of the conversation. .

CAROL: Okay. (long pause) One more thing... about Facebook. (beat) That's not how I deserved to learn about this.

LOU: You're right... I was trying to protect you and wait until the right time... But it all just got messed up, and I'm sorry for that.

CAROL: I just don't see why you need to let everyone into your business. People don't want to hear about all of this... None of this defines you...

LOU: Well, this is important to me. So, yeah, I'm gonna keep sharing and posting. I know who I am, and (sigh) you're right, this doesn't totally define me, but it defines where I feel safe. (long pause) I should go now. I'll think about the therapy, but only if you think about it too... Like I said, I'm excited about this and the way I'm evolving. If I were to be in therapy, it wouldn't be to know what my body needs; it would be to cope in this world where I am not believed.

CAROL: Okay.

LOU: Thanks for calling.

CAROL: I love you.

LOU: I love you too.

CAROL: Bye.

LOU: Bye.

# Chapter 8

# SOMETHING IN THE SODA

## MEGAN POIRIER

It's a Friday night, and the world is unraveling. It's November of 2013, so Armageddon is well past overdue. Despite mass paranoia, the Mayan calendar did not abruptly end the preceding year and neither did life as you know it. Yet, even if tonight will not be the end of the universe, your world has reached a precipice. You're teetering on the edge of an abyss that you know nothing about. Still, you never expect that Armageddon will arrive at a routine youth devotional in a vast, dimly lit auditorium with rafter seats. But you're 14 years old, so anything can happen.

The brick building is compact and unimposing. The fact that it contains a sprawling auditorium complete with rafters and an organ should be an impossibility. Towering pillars of white concrete stand guard on its front steps like cylindrical gargoyles. You wonder briefly—absurdly—if these pillars are angels, tasked with shielding any inhabitants within from harm. If they are angels, they certainly don't look the part. Then again, even angels start with *Do not be afraid*. The pair of rusted metal railings that flank the front steps appear even more out of place than the pillars. Nothing about this building screams *church*, unless you count the old organ that is decaying up in the rafters.

Most of this night will be erased from your mind. You remember it in strange fragments: a gray suit, rafters, soda. What details remain are sharp, but they exist in a bubble. It will take seven years for you to remember what city it happened in.

You have every reason to remember. Your dad has a new job in this city. When he clocks out of work, he meets you at the devotional down the street. That fact will become lost in a haze, unfiled for years. So will the fact that your mom attends the devo as well. It's a youth and family devotional, after all. She's sitting in the rafters with the dusty organ. You aren't with her, of course; you're too embarrassed to sit next to your mom in public. Though you know these things must be true, the memories are distorted. Fragments of reality glimpsed through a fishbowl, Polaroids scattered in the breeze.

You tell yourself, *At best, another Friday night devo will be an opportunity to talk with friends, connect with the God you've been taught to revere your whole life.* At worst, it will be beyond boring. There are never any warning signs that the world is crumbling around you. You are one of the youngest teenagers in attendance, and there is a multitude of things you don't know. You don't know how to prove you have a basic faith in God, the first requirement in the studying process before baptism. You don't know how to stop being an introvert, even though your mentors say you should. You don't know where you want to go to school, what you want to do. You don't know what you want in life. You don't know that your parents are briefed about the devotional beforehand. You don't know it's nothing factual, nothing honest. Like all disclaimers, it disclaims.

To parents, the church advertises the event as a multi-region devotional for teenagers. It's advertised as an educational opportunity for learning how to support members of the LGBTQ2S+ community. They claim that the devo will benefit any teenager who attends.

You climb the white steps and avoid the tetanus railings with hardly a care in the world. You enter that building as you've done countless Friday nights before. You may not know where you're going, but you see your finish line on the horizon, and you move toward it. Always moving. As you do so, you're met with the usual sea of young faces. A handful you know, and dozens you don't. You almost feel as if you're a speck of dust, a star within a constellation. Inconsequential and insignificant. How many feel the same?

The walls within the building are painted in shades of baby blue and beige, in alternating stripes. The center stage commands a powerful presence with its heavy navy-blue curtain. The stage is so high off the ground that it has its own mini staircase on the left side. As you choose your seat, you watch a man take to the stage. He introduces himself as the leader of a ministry within the church. He refers to himself as "ex-gay." You learn later that the term "leader" is accurate, as the ministry boasts hordes of those who have followed in his footsteps and become "ex-gay." They have borne their cross bravely, sacrificed their identities, and let Jesus in. Like ducklings, they will follow.

You have no way of knowing. You have never heard of this ministry or an "ex-gay" person before. You've hardly heard of a gay person. Yet, there you are anyway, a captive adolescent audience member. The curtain is up, and the masterpiece has begun.

The leader is sweating profusely that night out of sheer nerves, and he admits it. He stands behind the wooden podium in a hunched stance, wringing his hands, and says, "If I'm being honest, I'm very nervous about speaking to all of you tonight. I've spent a lot of time being embarrassed and ashamed of who I am."

He's dressed in a gray suit, as if for a funeral. If it is a funeral, it sure feels like yours. He makes all the attending teenagers play icebreaker games before his lesson, but you cringe. You don't want to hug three people next to you or say stupid encouraging things. Church games are beginning to feel humiliating and pointless. *We're always performing, always on display. From zero until the end of eternity.*

When the icebreakers dim to regretful embers, the message transforms into something unexpected, something impossible to prepare for. It's something that makes you pause as the gravity carrying you shifts into reverse.

Bile crawls up the back of your throat, slow and strange. Acid reflux is no stranger to you, but the sensation catches you off guard. Every cell stills as you curse your sensitive stomach. Now is not the time.

When you think of this night, you will always remember the poem "*Caged Bird*" by Maya Angelou. Fragments reverberate in your head like flakes in a snow globe. At first, you envision a powerful nightingale. It trills viciously for its freedom and uses its lungs with a vengeance. You repeat over and over, *the caged bird sings of freedom,* but you can't stop thinking about canaries. These nervous little birds stop singing when they sense that something's wrong. From coal mines to cats, every idiom hinges on their imprisonment. In every outcome, their music ceases. The whisper won't leave your mind.

The ex-gay leader nervously says, "I am a same-sex-attracted man. I led an actively homosexual lifestyle for many years, but I am also a happily married man now. My wife is an incredible woman, and I thank God for her. I'm here to tell all of you that there is hope. God opened my heart to fall in love with my wife. To change."

You don't know what to make of that. You had a gay uncle once, and the church always said it was a choice he made, a path he diverged on. One that killed him in the end. But you don't know why an important leader is here or what he's trying to say. It's a math problem you're entirely too exhausted to bother with. You trade a glance with one of your friends, but she doesn't know what to make of it either. The two of you are stumped, yet apprehensive. The teenagers surrounding you are silent in their contemplation. No one speaks, no one coughs, no one sneezes. You swear no one breathes.

The ex-gay leader says something that stops you in your muddled tracks completely. You swear your heart stops beating in that moment, the moment he declares, "I've been same-sex attracted my entire life, and I'm letting you know, having those feelings is not a choice." It's as if the crushing universe sways around you. The abyss has opened under your feet.

The abyss itself is unspeakable. You know it's there, but it takes all your energy to pretend that it isn't. So, you tell no one, not your relatives, not your friends. You're not brave enough to tell yourself, even in a whisper. You can't utter the full truth of it.

*Oh shit*, you think, *that explains so much.* You get a sensation like butterflies in your stomach but all wrong, all backwards. Maggots wriggling around in your guts, chewing their way out through your ribcage. It's the first time you've ever heard that "same-sex attraction" is not a choice. When all your peers began liking boys, you waited. You always thought that when you got your first period, you would fall head over heels for a guy. You waited and waited, but when it came it wasn't what you expected. You fell head over heels, but it wasn't for a boy. It was for a girl. Something in your brain clicks. You've been lured in by the leader's words. It seems almost like validation, but it's followed by a sucker punch.

The ex-gay leader hesitantly inspects the congregation of teenagers before him. The rafters loom above your head like teeth. The auditorium is almost cavernous in the dull light, and it easily seats over a hundred. It always does, at every teen devo. This one is no different. You hear him ask something outlandish like, "How much do you kids know about soda?"

You have even less of a clue where he's going in that instant. Nothing could predict it, really. He clarifies, "See, soda is actually really bad for you. I know that some of you probably like drinking it—it tastes good—but soda is actually really unhealthy for your body. As soon as you take that first sip, within ten minutes, the sugar in that soda goes right to your bloodstream, and it spikes your blood sugar levels. Acting on your same-sex attraction works in a very similar way. You might not be able to see it, but before you know it, that action adds up, and it's bad for you. It's not what God wants."

You remain rigid in your chair for the rest of his lesson.

The devo runs for two hours, as all devos do, but nothing else remains. Horror swallows you alive, until there's nothing left but that primal fear. Nothing left but the abyss.

After that night, you ask your parents to buy the ex-gay leader's book for you. He's written a series of them, for anyone aiming to live a God-fearing life as a same-sex-attracted Christian. Your mom is reluctant; she doesn't like the idea of paying money to access information. But you're insistent. The devo has provided answers to questions you hadn't known you were asking—but more importantly, you're scared. At 14, all you know is that reading that book and following in the footsteps of its author is the only way the church will ever baptize you. It's your only route to heaven. You must dip your toe into that abyss, let the darkness consume and then submerge you.

No one knows that in the years to follow, you fall to the floor, defeated, and pray for God to strip you of every feeling, everything that makes you human. You say, "Take all this away. Make me feel nothing. Make me nothing." You repeat quotes from *A Beautiful Mind*, ones you learned from the ex-gay leader. You replace the main character's schizophrenia with your own humanity and say, "I think that's what it's like with our emotions. We've got to keep feeding them for them to stay alive." You stop feeding them. It becomes its own kind of death, and within a month, you're diagnosed with major depression.

To your mentors, however, your "same-sex attraction" remains the larger problem. A fire to be snuffed out. When your mentors find out, it's not from your lips. Your parents spend your secrets as currency in an effort to save you. They're afraid, too. You blame yourself for telling them, chiding, "If only I had kept my mouth shut like a good little canary, this could have been avoided."

Your mentors ask you about sex, they ask about your silence, and you take it all for the sake of salvation. They say that to become a Christian, you must die to self. You must open yourself to the process, to vulnerability. He must become greater; you must become less. No matter the doubt, no matter the cost.

At first, thoughts of death are all you have to battle. But the memory begins to decompose within you and, as it does, infection sets in. What takes hold of your bloodstream then can only be defined as chaos. It's an incurable itch, this sensation that something within must be purged.

When the cycle begins, it's to rid yourself of the fear, the anger, and the shame, to both feel and be nothing. The first time it happens, you can feel a floodgate open. It's a floodgate you know you may never close again.

A wave of heat rushes through you, from your fingers to your toes. It is both a call to action and a command of paralysis. You sink to your knees before the toilet bowl, struck by its over-powering and pungent scent. Strands of saliva fall from your mouth as your esophagus prepares. It's hideous, and yet your knees are glued to the sticky tile floor. You don't have to shove your fingers down your throat or dry heave. There's none of that. There's no need.

The vomit comes whether you're ready or not.

# Chapter 9

# THE CALLING

## KIM KEMMIS

### Saturday

The night we arrived in San Diego, we saw aliens. We'd flown into LAX at 6 am from cold midwinter Sydney and taken the Amtrak down the coast to San Diego where the ex-gay conference was being held. We were hauling our bags up Broadway from the Santa Fe depot when we saw them, round green heads, big eyes, straight out of Roswell. I knew it had been a long day, and it was hot, and I was exhausted. But I couldn't be *that* exhausted. I nodded, they nodded back, and we all started to laugh. I like America, I decided.

In the hotel foyer, a sign welcomed people to Comic Con. "That explains the aliens," I said. Then M said, "Look," and pointed to another poster: *Welcome to San Diego Pride*. Really? Who schedules an ex-gay conference during Pride? By what arcane logic did they decide *that* was a good idea?

The hotel had opened in the 1920s, and from the outside, it certainly looked like it. But the website had assured us it had been renovated. Surprise number one: When we opened the door to our room, we realized we'd been put in the part that hadn't been refurbished. Surprise number two: no air conditioning. We sighed and put our bags down. I threw myself on the bed and grabbed the room guide. "It says here, this was the first hotel in San Diego to have ensuite bathrooms."

"Yeah, well," said M, "this ensuite doesn't have hot water."

I rang downstairs, and they assured me they'd get on it. I had a bracing cold shower, and we went out and found a restaurant for dinner.

That night I thought I would drop to sleep straight away, but as I was drifting off, I heard a loud "No…" from next door. "Go on," a male voice implored.

"*No!*" a female insisted.

"Baby, I've gotta get off…"

"Noooooo…"

There was a groan, then silence. Then M said, "These walls are pretty thin."

## Sunday

The hot water was back in the morning. We had planned to stay there for a night after the conference, but we canceled our booking and booked a luxury room in a nicer hotel around the corner.

We walked down Broadway and grabbed breakfast in a diner, and after a pleasant stroll back to the hotel, I threw up everything I had eaten.

"Should we give the Zoo a miss? We can stay here if you like," M offered.

"No. I'm not coming halfway around the world and missing the San Diego Zoo." We took the bus up to Balboa Park. I felt shaky. But I was determined, and once I was moving again, I felt better.

Then it began, in the queue for the pandas. It was so hot. I felt weak and had to hold onto the railing. I focused on the pandas. They lay unmoving in the shade. Poor pandas, having to live their lives in front of an audience, everyone thinking about how cute they look and how bad they are at breeding. It was like how they look at me in church. No, that was not helping at all.

After the pandas, we sat for a while under a shelter. I felt awful—so awful I had to cry. Was it the food, the heat, the exhaustion, the stress? M put her arm around me and stroked my shoulder while I quietly wept. I was concerned that people would stare, but they didn't. "It's okay," M said. "Depend on me. Depend on God." I got my act together, and we walked around the rest of the zoo, and I managed to have some lunch.

## Monday

The next morning, I brought up breakfast again. Then I started crying again. In a shopping center. Something ominous was coming, and I couldn't tell where or when. Back in the hotel, M helped me pack, item by item, folding each one and placing it carefully in the bag. One of my t-shirts had a white hair on it from our little cat, and my heart lurched. I missed him, and he was probably missing us. I found more of his hairs. I put them inside my Bible.

We'd planned to go by bus over to the university at Point Loma, but M decided we would take a cab. I didn't object. As we drove past the airport I watched the planes landing, one after the other. I had to get better. God had set me away for a purpose. Being here in America was part of that purpose. I knew God was going to tell me something about my life and my ministry. I couldn't listen and watch for that if I was crying and vomiting.

When we arrived at the university, we saw a banner across the building: *Into His Marvelous Light: 25th Exodus International North American Conference*. Right place. That was a plus. We registered and sat on the grass under a tree while we waited for our room assignment. A breeze came from the ocean, taking the edge off the heat. I felt much better. From somewhere we could hear a carillon playing hymns. Then came a tune I knew but couldn't place. Was it—no! Couldn't be. "Is that… *'Pretty Fly (For A White Guy)'*?"

M listened carefully. "Sounds like it." We laughed for the first time that day.

## Tuesday

Tuesday was the first *real* day of the conference. I had a good breakfast and kept it down. I could feel the anxiety still there, but I had it under control.

We went to the main chapel for the first plenary address, from one of the founders of Exodus. I'd met Frank Worthen the year before at an ex-gay leaders' conference in Brisbane. The stars of Exodus had been there: Frank, Bob Davies, the Director of Exodus North America, and Sy Rogers, the poster boy (or man) for ex-gay ministry. I'd even spent an afternoon by the pool with Sy talking about his career as a graphic designer for a defence contractor. That was a good conference; being a leader in an ex-gay ministry felt like I had finally come home. God had led me to a place where I could bring together the parts of me that conflicted, my faith and my sexuality, and make them work. It was okay to be bisexual, as long as I kept within the rules; and because I could talk about being bisexual, it felt as if I was breathing.

Today Frank talked about the early history of Exodus. "From the start, the message was 'Change is possible,'" he said. "Not 'Settle for celibacy.' And those of us who've changed must stand up and be seen, so that people can know we can change who we are." He had said the same thing in Brisbane, but it was important to hear it again. That's why I'm here, I thought. I've changed.

But in the queue for morning tea outside the commons I heard a man say, "I think change is overrated."

"It takes a long time," his friend assured him.

"Too long. I'm beginning to think it's not possible."

I thought, *You're not trying hard enough, pal.*

M and I found the library and sent an email to our supporters back home. *The flight was great, and we're enjoying America. We're getting used to summer again—the temperature is in the high*

*70s, and we're both a bit sunburned already. Kim has been having anxiety attacks and feeling unwell but seems to be on the mend.*

The replies came back quickly. *You're under attack from the Evil One*, a friend wrote, *but we will pray for you to find God's perfect peace.* I don't think it's the Evil One, I thought, more likely exhaustion. But thanks for the peace.

Lunch and dinner stayed down, and I celebrated by getting a book signed by John Paulk. John was another big shining light: He had been gay, married a former lesbian, and had two kids, and now he was the Exodus board chairman. I'd told him I'd really enjoyed his autobiography, *Not Afraid to Change*, because it was a little racier than most of the ex-gay memoirs. John laughed and signed my book.

"Nice man," I said to M. It had been a good day. Three full meals, and all of it where it should be.

## Wednesday

The next morning, we breakfasted with some people from San Jose, very friendly cat lovers, who gave us a standing invitation to stay over if we were ever up that way. We were finding that Americans are quite friendly. They offer so much of their souls without requiring commitment; they may never see you again after you finish lunch.

"There's a make-up workshop this morning," M noted.

"That's for the lesbians. You a lesbian?"

"No."

"Didn't think so. You know how to do make-up." I saw the newspaper dispenser and peered through the glass to see what had been happening out in the world. No. My favourite plane, ever since I was a kid. "Shit!"

"What?"

"Concorde crashed."

"What?"

"Concorde has crashed. In Paris. After take-off. All dead." I felt the anxiety tug at me again. I felt a long way from home.

We went up to the main chapel for the morning's plenary with Andy Comiskey of Desert Stream. He talked about celibacy, too. "Gay celibacy is not the spiritual gift of celibacy," he declared. "It's an accommodation to brokenness. To be true to your humanity you have to learn to relate to the opposite sex."

*Which is hard*, I thought.

"But that's also the goal of heterosexual people," he continued.

Of course. It's hard for everyone. I hoped the guy in yesterday's queue was listening.

After lunch, M and I did our laundry, then split up for the afternoon workshops. I went to one on "Developing A Secure Gender Identity." You need to step out of your comfort zone in accepting your gender identity, they said. Accepting your gender identity. Not changing it. Not necessarily the message for me. I hadn't really been challenged in my gender identity; I'd always liked being a man, or at least trying to be the kind of man I thought I should be. But it was something I could use to help the guys in my group.

That night we had a "Mexican fiesta" in the amphitheatre,

basically a big barbecue with sombreros. I wore a Hawaiian shirt, out by a few thousand miles but still festive. A violin and guitar played Mexican-sounding music. We ate our barbecue, and I told M about the afternoon's workshop. "It's interesting," I said. "They were talking about 'gender wholeness.' They weren't saying, 'Change, change, change,' like everyone else. It was more like... don't think of it as change; think of it as becoming what you already are."

"Did they say that?"

"No. Not specifically, no."

Maybe they didn't mean that. I gazed at the ocean, watched a submarine sailing slowly up the coast. Maybe there was another way of reading it, but my belly was full, and the music started again, and I thought that I should just relax and enjoy the evening.

A group of people walked into the arena and began line dancing, a line of five, and a line of three. Then one man came out and danced behind them, a line of his own. The audience laughed and clapped. They were very good. As the dancers took their bows and walked off, the P.A. crackled, and there was an announcement. "Sorry, but no more dancing. University rules. Exodus will get fined." We almost choked on our churros. *Line dancing?* Fair enough, a Christian university, no drinking or smoking. But how can you get a thousand queers together and not let them dance?

The man who'd danced on his own came out again and stood in the middle of the arena, looking solemn, like a chastened child. Gradually all the other dancers came out and stood with him, a line of hangdogs. Then slowly they began to wheel around, half a circle one way, half a circle the other. Then they stopped and very discreetly tapped their right feet. Everyone broke up.

"That's not dancing," M said.

"No, that's repentance," I agreed.

## Thursday

On Thursday morning, we had an early start, a 7 am breakfast meeting with Pat Lawrence, the International Coordinator for Exodus. I'd met her in Brisbane, too. A bunch of us had gone to a bar after the leaders' meetings, not realizing it was a lesbian bar until after the second drink. Instead of fleeing from sin as good Christians should, we laughed hysterically and ordered another round. I mentioned our mutual friend Natalie, another ministry leader who'd been in the bar with us. Pat's usually happy face changed. "I'm so angry with her," she said. "And disappointed. I thought we'd settled all the issues. We talked so much about it."

This was all new. "Sorry. What happened with Nat?"

"Didn't you know? She's pulled her group out of Exodus."

"Wow. Why did she do that?"

"Because she doesn't think people can change. It wasn't happening for them, so she's decided it's wrong."

I was at a loss for words. "I know," Pat said, shaking her head.

We spent the next hour talking about business, but I'd really been thrown by the news about Natalie. M and I attended the morning sessions, but we were exhausted. After lunch, we headed back down to our room. I sat by the window and watched a squirrel playing in the long grass behind the dorm building. I could feel the anxiety lurking just out of sight, threatening to upset the balance I'd worked so hard to get back. I tried to think of some Bible verses, looked for something that could reassure me, God's saving grace and all that. But it was better just to sit and breathe deeply. On Saturday, it would be all over, and we could go on our holiday and relax.

### Friday

We'd run out of things to say during meals and gave ourselves permission not to go to a session if we really didn't need to. But we made sure we went to the Friday reception. Like the other party it was held outside in the warm summer night. We grabbed some (non-alcoholic) drinks and took up station near a sculpture, a life-sized bronze of Jesus and Peter entitled *The Calling*. A stranger approached us. "Where are you from?"

"Australia."

"I *thought* so! I love your accent!"

"Thank you."

"Say something."

"Ummm... It's lovely to be here in the U.S., people have been so friendly, and we're having a great time."

"Wow! Say something else."

I searched for something profound, but all I could think of was a couple of lines from *The Man from Snowy River*, a poem I can't stand:

There was movement at the station, for the word had passed around

That the colt from Old Regret had got away.

"Great! Say 'G'day.'"

I don't say "G'day," and neither do most of my countrymen. We'd already got past the greeting stage, so I was at a loss for the right context. I looked around and saw the sculpture, noticed that Jesus's hand extended at just the right level. I grasped it and shook it. "G'day, Jesus," I said. "Love your work."

The man gasped as if I had blasphemed, then shook his head slowly. "You Australians," he said. "Your humor..." He moved away.

I realised M was laughing. "Got rid of him."

It had, but now I was irritated. He was friendly and then passed judgement. Why was I annoyed? I should be used to it. I looked at the party going on around us, and I felt detached from all these nice Christians. I don't belong with these people, I thought. They're not my kind.

## Saturday

I woke up feeling discontented but blamed it on the tiredness. It had been a long week.

After the final worship session in the morning, we waited for our cab outside the chapel. We were exchanging email addresses with a new friend when I became aware of raised voices. "If you can't change, you're not trying." Heads turned toward two men, side by side but now moving to face each other.

"Everyone's saying it now," the second man said. "It isn't possible."

"No!" the first man shouted. The two men were face to face; their bodies seemed set for violence. I readied myself to intervene when a calm but firm voice called out, "Guys, settle down." It was Bob Davies. He placed a hand on each man's shoulder and spoke quietly to them. Everyone looked away and went back to their farewells, a little disturbed.

Our taxi passed through the gates of the university back into the big wide world. The air conditioning caressed our faces like a blessing. I exhaled deeply, letting all the air go out of me. We sat in silence.

I changed, I thought. I'm proof we can change. Yes, it had been hard. The times I'd been prayed over and demons cast out of me, the discipline I'd forced on myself not to look, not to think, not to act. But I'd changed.

Or had I? Maybe I had just stopped doing the bad stuff and thought I had changed. Maybe it's easier because I'm bisexual and married.

If we can't *really* change—if I'm wrong—my career is gone, my ministry, or what was left of it after coming clean about my sexuality. What if my marriage is wrong, everything I've worked for... I felt the anxiety rise again.

No, absurd. They're mistaken. I took M's hand.

The taxi dropped us off at the nice hotel. We hoped for a good night's sleep; tomorrow was another early start, because

we were flying to Las Vegas to renew our marriage vows
with Elvis.

Chapter 10

# THE BOY WHO DANCED FOR GOD'S GENERAL

## JONATHON SAWYER

A militant celebrity preacher I once revered—whom I referred to as "God's General"—claimed to possess a spiritual anointing that gave him the ability to smell "homosexual demons." I was 16 years old when I first read about the preacher's keen spirit-smelling ability. He wrote about it in a book on haunted houses, ghosts, and demons. Around the same time, while listening to one of his sermons on cassette tape, I anxiously heard his impassioned voice, with a hint of Southern twang, preach that his "gift" was strongest while casting out evil spirits from individuals who the Holy Ghost helped him identify as in need of "deliverance." The crowd was electrified. I was enchanted and, secretly, hopeful. Could all my confusion, self-doubt, and self-revulsion be fixed under his anointing? Not long thereafter, I too would smell a homosexual demon—revolted by the stench of God's General atop my body during a public session of violent exorcism.

My star-struck admiration of God's General lasted from about age 9 to 21. During those years, he was a rising celebrity in the Pentecostal Word of Faith movement. He earned early fame by regaling adoring crowds with a fantastical tale about how he had been personally transported to heaven at eight years of age. As a prepubescent boy, I was particularly enthralled with his stories about heaven's golden streets, flowers of vivid colors that constantly transformed, lush green grass that never withered, and his water fight with Jesus in the River of Life.

When I was 17, God's General visited a local church in my area. It was my first time seeing him in person, and the first time he knocked me to the ground—in a prayer line that Pentecostals call being "slain in the Spirit." I nervously laughed during his sermon, "Does Your Pastor Carry a Knife?" in which he made jabbing motions at the audience while holding a sharp blade. At the climax of the sermon, he demanded that people in the audience not become "homos" or "lezzies." At this event, God's General promoted his now defunct Spirit Life Bible College in Orange County, California. Enamored at the prospect of a new life pursuing the high calling of God, I applied. On the application—and with trepidation but conviction—I divulged my "struggle with same-sex attraction." I believed God's General was a prophet and thus could perceive any lie of omission on my application. I was, of course, certain to clarify that I was not "committed to the homosexual lifestyle." I was admitted and enrolled. In due time, God's General paid for me to attend counseling sessions that were aimed at "healing" my experiences of same-sex attraction. Those sessions would come after other methods failed.

At Spirit Life Bible College, gatherings of the student body were held in the megachurch affiliated with the school. The sanctuary was richly designed with teal carpet and plush navy-blue chairs. The stage wall was adorned with a maroon arch under which a three-dimensional map of the world was prominently displayed: an ocean of midnight black, turquoise continents, and an encircling flame of fire. The first week of class was called "Clean Out Week"—five days set aside for students to receive deliverance from the demons we brought with us to the school. Clean Out Week was the stuff of legends: I had heard stories of possessed men levitating off the ground, of women demonstrating demonically inspired (and masculine-coded) strength, and of all forms of satanic shackles broken by the power of the Holy Ghost. I desperately wanted my same-sex desires vanquished from my heart and mind, and I believed that God's General had the power to help me achieve that goal.

The worship band fervently played a thunderous song of spiritual warfare. Drums were beaten with hypnotic frenzy. Electric guitars were fiercely strummed. Keyboards were passionately banged. With peculiar expressions of agitated joy, the singers belted out repetitive lyrics that were accompanied by a boisterous yet sinister melody in a minor key. In a black pantsuit, the band's worship leader aggressively paced the stage. With sweat percolating and smearing the makeup on her contorted face, she screamed in tongues and spat ecstatic utterances. She boldly declared heavenly victory over a host of wicked spirits.

*The heavens are opening!*

Sixty students bolted from their seats to the church altar— cacophonous voices pleading for divine deliverance. In an aggrandized posture, God's General authoritatively walked on the stage and quickly dominated it with his fleshy presence. As the band continued to play, he coarsely shouted warfare prayers while kicking into the air at the malevolent spiritual forces in the room. God's General fanned the unrestrained flames of our youthful passion, the growing intensity of an imminent battle with a legion of demonic forces. I stood among my comrades in spiritual arms: hands outstretched, neck straining toward the heavens, and with tears streaming down my clenched face. I could taste the forthcoming freedom, and I pleaded with the Lord for his intervention through God's General. I needed his powerful touch. Remarkably, my earnest desire came true. Suddenly, God's General leaped from the stage and slammed my forehead.

I tumbled to the ground.

In shock and awe, I laid with God's General directly on my chest. As the intensity of the band's warfare song grew, he shouted incantations of spiritual deliverance over me. I observed a gold chain around his neck and noted his profusely hairy chest. I also inhaled a pungent witch's brew of sour body odor and sticky-sweet cologne. God's General became uncomfortably heavy, but I briefly felt a sense of potent privilege to be in this position of subjugation to the prophet of God. This was the moment I would be free of these cursed same-sex attractions. Yet, bewilderingly, God's General exuded a tenacious, sexual energy. It was a powerful, though not enjoyable, exertion of maniacal control. As the preacher's weight became almost unbearable, I struggled to be free.

Then, I left my body.

I could see from a bird's eye view God's General on my chest. I experienced a moment of compassion and concern for the boy under his domain. I wanted out of this twisted role play. But the prophet persisted. Then, while continuing to shout into the void that was growing in my soul, God's General summoned his men with a hasty gesture. Several eager henchmen (whom God's General called "armor bearers") assumed their excited positions over me. As God's General was anchored on my chest, spitting in my face at the demons in my soul, his armor bearers forced and held each one of my limbs—arms and legs—to the ground. The initial honor I felt as a captive of the prophet had turned into palpable horror. This was a stained altar.

Out of thin air, a voice emerged from my body that I did not recognize. The demon voice spewed a litany of wretched words. In a distorted, high, and scratchy pitch, "the demon" screeched at God's General.

*"You liar!"*

*"You fucker!"*

*"You... false... prophet!"*

A river of rage coursed swiftly through my veins: a visceral hatred for this putrid performance of piety, this unrelenting quest for a state of elusive inner purity. God's General responded with a deep and gravelly shout of unhinged authority. He commanded the unclean spirit to "COME OUT OF HIM IN THE NAME OF JESUS!"

I continued to play the role, screaming at God's General and damning him to the hell in which I believed, to the hell I was experiencing. God's General became impossibly heavy as he continued to exert his weight on my chest, eventually obstructing my airway. The demonic profanity spewing from my mouth turned into the very human plea of a deeply impressionable boy.

"I can't breathe," I tried to say.

"I can't breathe," I said.

I could not breathe.

Finally, I felt the oppressive weight and the foul, sweaty stench of God's General lift.

*Am I free?*

No. I was paralyzed. I remained on the floor of that diabolical altar, face toward the ceiling, eyes closed, hair tousled, freshly dried tears on my blood-red cheeks. Stunned. I heard no sound, but I sensed the searing glares of anticipation from my fellow classmates. They were awaiting my rise to a newfound liberation. Aching vibrations of confusion throbbed through my bones.

As I tepidly opened my eyes in dreary shame, the once vibrant colors of the sanctuary had devolved into dull hues of smoldering brown with layers of decaying grey. A rotten, orange, translucent haze enveloped every object and every person in the room. After a dazed and silent eternity, the sound of the worship band gradually returned to my ears. The sound grew into a violent echo. Energized by the thumping, ascending lines of an electric bass guitar, all the people sang: "When I think about Jesus, and what he's done for me; when I think about Jesus, and how he's set me free, I want to dance, dance, dance, dance, dance, dance, dance all day!"

*Is it time to get up?*

I couldn't. I needed to stay lying on the ground, safely encased in a coffin of culpability for all that was wrong with me, and for all that was wrong in the world. It was a massive weight that I could not possibly endure, and yet thought I must endure. I closed my eyes.

Then somehow—and I don't quite know how—I did what was expected of me. Shaking off the initial shock, but still stupefied, I managed to get up from the floor. Then, as if I were a computer that was programmed to fight off a menacing virus, I tried to dance off the corruption. I contorted into painful gyrations of gleeful melancholy. I kicked with an anxious jolt of my right leg, like God's General kicked, into chaos and confusion. I whirled like a dervish beset by devils. My fellow classmates shouted with a collective voice of triumph, awed in their belief that I danced freely like David danced before the ark of the Lord.

I had changed inside—but I would soon learn that what had changed was not my attraction to men. The joyous and anticipatory hope of a better world with sweet Jesus was replaced with a performance of bitter survival. I fended off an army of happily fanged ghouls in a heavenly graveyard of feigned victory. I danced at the horror of who I was and who I feared I might never become.

Again, I left my body.

I experienced a revelation that I only began to understand many years later. I was a disembodied spirit occupying another dimension of time and space within the sanctuary. I stood near God's General at the far side of the room. Then, I entered him. For a moment, I possessed his vision and experienced his feelings. I, God's General, was agitated and felt thoroughly depleted of energy. With dead eyes, I, God's General, noticed an indistinguishable collection of students at the foot of the church altar. The distance between me, God's General, and the students was insurmountable, like the gulf between the rich man in hell who vainly pleaded to heaven for just one dip of cool water on his parched tongue. Then, I, God's General, focused my vision on the dancing boy.

He was just coming into manhood, with a tall and robust frame—the height and weight of a football quarterback. Yet, he appeared small and feeble. His khaki pants were stained. His scratchy, red polo shirt was shredded and dangling from his body. He was branded by a burning coal that seared the side of his face: guilt not taken away, sin not forgiven. Dark chasms encircled his furrowed brow. Ashes of the damned were smeared on his forehead. As the boy danced, he bowed his head in dejected submission to the preacher who preyed on men. God's General looked at the boy with curious, contemptuous arousal. The boy was the workmanship of his hands, performing just as he desired.

I had become a fearful, shaking, Pentecostal corpse.

## Chapter 11

# INTO THE DARK

## CHRIS CSABS

The applause of the church congregation was drowned out by the thumping music from the speakers. My shirt clung to my body, the sweaty fabric testifying to the heat that bore down from the stage lights. Smiling brightly, I strode off the stage toward the wings, out of sight of the audience.

"Nice one, guys," said Tori, our lead vocalist.

"Thanks," I said, sighing and dropping my microphone into a black zip-bag and wiping my forehead with a cloth. I let my smile fall, resting my cheeks before I'd have to use them again. I relaxed my shoulders, allowing them to drop slightly. For the last hour, I had been "on," deliberately holding myself in a way that I thought was more masculine than my natural stance.

The other three singers who remained on stage jumped happily off the front of the platform, loudly thanking the pastor for having us and greeting the small groups of worshippers who stood waiting to catch one of us for a conversation. I sat down on one of the large black speakers. I needed a moment to drum up the energy to do as the others did with such ease. I could never really relax around people we met "on the road." I had a secret that required constant effort to maintain. No one would want to meet me without my mask on.

When I was auditioning for my place in the band, it was noted that the way I moved was problematic. Apparently, I had been suspected as gay immediately. There were a number of things that had given me away, including the sound of my voice in conversation and the tilt of my head when listening. This suspicion had necessitated an in-depth explanation of my journey as a Christian before I could be accepted as an official part of the band's ministry.

Over the past four years, a towering question mark had been placed over my childhood and my relationship with my parents, as I was assisted to find the part of me that was faulty, the cause of my same-sex attraction. I had tried everything to find the root of my problem in order to fix it, from Christian counseling to a group program run out of a church for people struggling with their "broken sexualities." I had even tried a deliverance ministry, where demons were commanded to come out of my body as I sat with my palms facing skyward, silently begging God to answer my prayers. Nothing so far had worked.

At the time, I felt lucky to be officially accepted into the band, despite having what was considered such a shameful problem.

"Hey, man!"

Instinctively, I squared my shoulders at the sound of the voice before turning to see a blonde, messy-haired guy in his early twenties. His naturally athletic frame looked relaxed, his sun-bronzed skin and faded t-shirt adding to the impression that this was somebody who floated effortlessly through life. He was smiling broadly at me. I couldn't help but notice his incredibly large blue eyes.

*God, help me!*

I stood quickly and forced a smile. "Thanks a lot," I said, momentarily losing my "straight guy" posture as I quickly became flustered.

*No, Chris. You are a new creation in Christ. Straighten up!*

He stuck a toned arm out to shake my hand as I squared my shoulders further. There were his eyes again, looking at me kindly.

*Don't look at him!*

I deliberately moved my eyes past him, hoping he wouldn't notice or think I was being rude. Everything in me wanted to engage normally with this man, but it felt dangerous, as if being present with him in the moment would constitute a choice contrary to my new life as a soon-to-be straight man. I took his hand and shook it, outdoing the strength in his grip. I then let my hand drop and pretended to be suddenly interested in picking some fluff off my shirt, so that I could continue to avoid looking at his face. Aware that I was coming across as odd, I again allowed my eyes to meet his.

*What if this is feeding my homosexuality, making it stronger?*

I felt panic rising as the thoughts in my head grew louder.

*You're opening the door to Satan!*

"I'm Scott. So great to have you here at our church!" he beamed. "You guys were fantastic—you must love what you do!"

For a moment, I thought about responding honestly. What could I tell him? Traveling the country and singing like this probably looked like the best job in the world, but in reality, I had little ability to truly enjoy it.

"Hey, I'm Chris," I said, smiling. "Yeah, it's a lot of fun."

Sweat began to bead on my forehead again. I moved my gaze downwards, this time pretending to be interested in one of the speaker cables on the floor that I began pushing to the side with my foot.

*Get out of here!*

"Hey, I'm really sorry, Scott," I sputtered, "I've got to get all this equipment packed up and back on the bus. Can I catch you later?"

A momentary look of confusion flashed across his face before he nodded. "Of course, no problem! Bless ya, bro!" he replied cheerfully, bringing his long arms out in a bear-like hug, seemingly unaware of my discomfort. My heart instantly started beating faster.

*I'm disgusting.*

I returned the hug briefly, acutely aware in that moment that, because of my plan to become straight, this would probably be the most physical affection that I'd ever again have with another man. My heart ached, and I intentionally turned my attention to the view I had of the others, still mingling and laughing with the swelling group of other congregants. Without hesitating, I let my arms drop and quickly turned, lifting up the speaker and walking it around the back of the stage toward the exit door. My head was spinning. Had I sinned just now? Or, even worse, had I just taken a step backward in my recovery?

Outside, the night air was cool, making the hair on my arms stand on end. I briskly walked the speaker over to our tour bus and set it on the ground. The sound of laughter and music was still coming from inside the doorway. I needed to be somewhere alone and quiet. I fumbled for my keys and unlocked the door to the bus, sliding it open and stepping inside. It was dark, but I didn't turn on the light. I needed to hide for a few minutes. I pushed aside the curtain that concealed our bunk beds and stumbled past the array of clothing and bags to find the seat at the very back of the bus behind another black curtain. Pulling it behind me, I created a space the size of a small wardrobe.

I sat for a moment while my eyes adjusted to the near complete darkness. Eventually I could make out the folds of the curtain, a thin sliver of light peeking through. My mind was muddled, and my limbs felt heavy. I wanted to clench my fists into balls and scream in frustration and anger at my inability to simply be *normal* like the others.

I had enjoyed that hug, as brief as it was. As I sat and thought about my perversion, I started to feel physically dirty, an uncomfortable churning beginning in my stomach. These days, I was so strict with myself—I was hypervigilant about where my eyes went, the people I spoke to. It had been several years since I had held a man's hand, kissed his lips. I had very rarely even let my eyes linger on an attractive face. Interacting with any man around my own age often felt like I was playing with fire.

I took a deep breath and let the air out slowly. "Go away in the name of Jesus!" I breathed fiercely into the dark, my voice shaking. "I bind that sexual attraction in the name of Jesus, and I send it to the foot of the cross!" I was repeating the same words uttered by a pastor during a previous attempt to rid me of demonic attachments.

Praying this just once didn't seem enough to ensure I had sufficiently repented. I spent the next several minutes praying, begging God to forgive and heal me. I still felt dirty, noticing my sweaty skin prickling beneath my jeans. I would need to shower immediately when we got back to our accommodation, even though it would be difficult. I had started becoming distressed by having to touch my own body, as though even washing myself could be a sinful act that was somehow connected to the evil that plagued me. Showers needed to be quick and often ended with a silent prayer for forgiveness in case I had inadvertently sinned while washing myself. I was hypersensitive to bodily sensations, spending many minutes and sometimes hours a day silently asking God to forgive me for noticing things like the tickle of the tag at the back of my underwear, all while my bandmates loudly wondered why I was sitting at the back of the bus on my own with my eyes closed and a frown on my face. Even at that moment, the sensation of my damp shirt against my skin felt somehow connected to my filthy sinfulness, and I added this into my prayers for forgiveness.

I continued to sit in the dark, knowing that my absence wouldn't go unnoticed for much longer. I had to make this quick, but I couldn't rush the prayers so that they were ingenuine. I tried to concentrate, picturing myself sitting before Jesus, physically handing him a box containing my sexual immorality, my evil bodily sensations, my homosexual attraction. "Take it, Lord," I breathed.

My prayers were interrupted by the sound of footsteps and voices outside. This had taken longer than I thought. As they grew closer, I recognized the voices of my bandmates.

"Where's Chris?" said Tori, sounding mildly frustrated.

"Dunno," replied the deeper voice of our sound man. "Probably in the bus—he has the key."

My stomach dropped. Hurriedly, I flung the curtain aside and moved through the bus, uncomfortably aware of the tingling sensation on my skin from sitting for too long in one position. Holding the cold metal of the handle, I took a deep breath before heaving the sliding door open.

"Oh, hey guys!" I said, jumping from the doorway and once again stretching my mouth into a smile.

"What were you doing in there?" said Tori, frowning.

I couldn't explain it to them. I knew it wasn't normal. I wished I could make them understand, but I knew they couldn't. I tried to brush the question off instead.

"What do you mean? I just started packing up!" I responded, picking up the speaker I had left on the ground and carrying it around to the trailer attached to the back of the bus.

Tori let me know that she was disappointed I had taken time to myself while the rest of them were still working. The most important part of our ministry was the connections we made with people, not our on-stage performance.

"We are all tired, Chris," Tori said before walking back toward the open door of the church hall.

Following her inside a minute later, I noticed that the music had stopped and that the hall lights had been turned on. People had moved into smaller groups, most of them having cheerful conversation peppered with loud laughter. Young guys slapped each other's backs, guffawing at jokes and making faces at each other. Couples stood close to each other, guys with their arms draped around their girlfriends' shoulders or hugging them from behind. Some families with children had begun rounding them up, readying them to leave.

I stood alone next to the stage, surveying the scene. My eyes briefly clocked Scott talking with Tori and the others, a large smile plastered across his face as they all connected so effortlessly.

I took a step towards them.

*No.*

Frowning and shaking my head slightly, I paused. Bending down, I picked up the long, black cable that I had been pushing aside with my foot only minutes earlier and began looping it over my arm. The sound of the laughter again tempted to lure my attention. Scott's light-hearted laugh was louder than the others. I tightened my grip on the cord, coiling it round and round my arm, focusing on the weight of it increasing with every loop.

With a deep breath I shifted my weight, heaving the now-bundled cable over my left arm while picking up a microphone stand with my right hand. The sound of laughter slowly faded as I walked back outside into the dark.

# Chapter 12

# DELIVER US FROM EVIL

## RICK DANIELSON

"Tell us your name!"

I opened my mouth, hoping the right word would slip out. Nothing. "Homosexuality?" I suggested, hoping the obvious was correct. It wasn't.

Two figures hovered over me; one was a seminary professor, the other a pastor. The professor addressed the evil spirits again, more forcefully: *"What is your name?!"* Still nothing.

The pastor helping with the ritual left the room and returned with a soda can filled with water from the hallway fountain.

Sweat formed on my brow as the session continued. My breaths became shallow and rapid. My fingers tingled and felt numb. I reported the sensation and was told: "It's because of what you did with your hands."

The tingling, the professor explained, was a spiritual manifestation of my sin. I had touched men in a sexual manner, and now my hands revealed the terrible truth. Everything suddenly felt very "real," and I was terrified. One of the men threw water at my head, and a loud, anguished cry escaped from me. I sobbed for a few minutes as tears washed over my face. It seemed like a breakthrough, like something was finally happening. Perhaps the demons had come out. I began to breathe easier, and my racing heartbeat slowed. The tingling in my hands diminished and then disappeared.

A few days earlier, I had met with the pastor who would later host the exorcism in his office. He was a gentle, kind man who listened to my angst with concern. I was living on the campus of the seminary I attended for one year to complete coursework for a doctoral degree while taking a break from pastoral ministry. The year was nearing an end, and I would soon leave with my wife and small children for a new church assignment. Few people knew my secret; for decades I had struggled with same-sex desires, which led me to act out in ways contrary to who I understood myself to be. Over and over, I had begged God to make me normal.

During an earlier degree program at the same school, I participated in numerous sessions of "inner healing prayer," asking Jesus to heal the wounds from childhood that resulted in my so-called sexual confusion as an adult. A few years before that, the director of counseling services at my church-related college referred me to a reparative therapist when I sought help. The therapist explained that I had never properly bonded with my father as a child. My attraction to men was a sexualized attempt to "repair" the relationship with my dad. Even though I thought I had a good relationship with him, I learned that it couldn't possibly be so. My relationship with my father deteriorated as one Christian counselor after another, over 17 years, persuaded me that he had failed to truly love me.

Now in my late thirties, I told the pastor in whom I confided that the only thing I hadn't tried to rid myself of homosexual desires was demonic deliverance: exorcism. Though I had occasionally scoffed at those who saw demonic activity behind every human struggle, I was desperate to put this long chapter of my life behind me. The pastor shared that there was one respected person in the community who was able to perform such a ritual. Coincidentally, as it turned out, he was also my dissertation advisor. I weighed the possibility that confession might prevent me from attaining my doctorate with the intense desire to be free of my besetting sin. Without hesitation, I agreed for the pastor to set up the exorcism. Nothing mattered more to me right then than being free.

Three days later, I set off on foot for my appointment at the pastor's office. His church met in a big barn-like structure at a campground just outside town. Hundreds of students and faculty and townspeople gathered each Sunday for a pep rally-like service with a loud band and energetic singing and preaching. The service ended most weeks with people coming down the aisle to surrender their lives to Jesus and be "slain in the Spirit." The church offices were elsewhere, in the center of town. As I walked down the sidewalk in that direction, memories of my childhood raced through my mind.

My family was active in the Charismatic Movement of the 1970s. There was a lot of talk of demons then, and it seemed to me that demons lurked around every corner. I took to rebuking them as a regular habit, and it was easy for me at an early age to blame any of my shameful thoughts on them. When I was a pre-teen, just beginning to experience my sexual awakening, I read a book that my parents had purchased and left on a coffee table. It was about demons and the influence they can have on Christians. A chapter on homosexuality caught my attention because it touched on my deepest and scariest secret: Unlike my buddies, I was attracted to boys instead of girls. I read that demons were not capable of fully possessing Christian believers but that evil spirits could still enter and "oppress" them if allowed. Around that time, my older brother was diagnosed with schizophrenia. While my parents sometimes attributed his illness to demons, they weren't entirely certain what caused it, and they visited him weekly in the hospital where he was heavily medicated. One Saturday, while they traveled the several hours to and from the hospital, I followed the instructions for self-exorcism that I found in the book on the living room table. I lay on the cool concrete floor of our basement because the book said that demons could come out as a slimy substance and I didn't want to ruin the carpet in my bedroom. I commanded the evil spirits to leave, several times, and nothing happened. I figured I was just a kid and probably did it wrong. Decades later, walking down the street near my seminary and waving hello to friends, I was off to see a bonafide exorcist, so it could be done properly.

I arrived at the nondescript building that housed the church offices. A secretary greeted me with a tight smile, and I wondered if she knew why I was there. Was "exorcism" listed on the staff schedule for the day? I sat nervously in the waiting area for several minutes until directed to the pastor's office. The seminary professor who held my academic future in his hands was already there. I felt embarrassed and awkward, but he greeted me warmly and directed me to sit in a chair facing the two men. I was asked some direct questions about my sexual history and answered them truthfully. The professor spoke with kindness, reminding me of God's forgiveness. He also told me about the power of "generational curses" and pondered what evils in my family history resulted in demonic influence and perversion.

We proceeded with an extended time of silent and spoken prayer, and then my professor addressed the demons: "You have no authority here! You have no power over this child of God, and you must leave in the name of Jesus!"

The demons were then instructed to announce their names, and I realized that I was on the spot. After all the preparation for this moment, I needed to do the right thing. I had no idea, though, what to do or what should happen. Was I supposed to be a passive vessel of some sort, with demons opening and twisting my mouth to force out guttural utterances? Or would the demonic names be revealed in my mind, so that I could just relay them to the others in the room? Images of Linda Blair in *The Exorcist* popped into my head, and the pressure I felt to play my part well was intense. I had been told to report any physical sensations that I might be feeling, and so I did. I was shocked and felt deeply ashamed when told that the buzzing feeling in my hands was related to the body parts of the men I had touched. It wasn't enough to just confess my sin; my body had to announce my shame as well.

When the session was over, despite the disappointment that no demons had identified themselves by name, I was given photocopied instructions on what to do and how to pray, so that I would remain demon-free. I was told to purchase a workbook written by a noted deliverance minister with further instructions for "aftercare." I passed the church secretary on my way out and wondered how much of the wailing she had heard from her desk.

Walking home after what I later came to think of as my soda-can deliverance session, I felt confused and conflicted. Was it all real? Was *any* of it real? In retrospect, most of what I experienced had seemed contrived and exhausting. It didn't take long for me to realize that the tingling sensation in my hands was caused by hyperventilation. I noticed a handsome college student cross the street ahead of me. He looked as if he worked out a lot, and I instantly hated that I noticed. Couldn't I be free for even ten whole minutes?! I wondered why God wouldn't deliver me and whether I wasn't trying hard enough or hadn't surrendered myself fully. Submitting to the exorcism had felt like a risky last resort. No one pressured me to do it; it was voluntary. Why wouldn't God honor my intentions, however imperfect, and finally help me?

The day after the deliverance appointment, I returned to the church office and met one-on-one with the pastor. During the exorcism, he had sort of faded into the background; now it was just the two of us. He seemed a bit hesitant as he spoke: "Um, how are you doing today?"

"Doing okay, thanks. I guess I'm still processing yesterday."

"I understand. I've been doing the same. To be really honest, I'm not entirely comfortable with everything that happened."

"Really? I've had some serious doubts, too, but have been trying to talk myself out of them."

The conversation continued as we tried to make sense of it all. I expressed my near certainty that the cries and tears, and the tingling, were something other than a spiritual breakthrough. He couldn't disagree, and our meeting was brief. I sensed that he regretted his involvement in the deliverance session. We parted without a plan to speak again, and we never did. I was grateful for the reassurance that my doubts were okay.

Three years later, after I made the decision to come out as a gay man, I wrote to the professor who rebuked my demons. I let him know that while I was grateful for his concern about my soul, I was choosing a new path. I planned to be back on campus soon for the funeral of a beloved spiritual mentor, and I asked the professor if I could see and speak with him in person. He did not reply to my letter. At the funeral, I saw that he was seated right behind me. At the conclusion of the service, I turned around to greet him and to ask if he had received my letter.

"Yes," he replied. Then: "I'm disappointed."

With that, he turned his back to me, walked the length of his church pew, and exited the church. I never saw or heard from him again.

# Chapter 13

# EXODUS OF SHAME

## SYRE KLENKE

I had never felt so alone as I did that week in 2009. I was surrounded by nearly a thousand people in an auditorium at Wheaton College. The air was thick and heavy with the collective weight of desperation. Each breath felt like a struggle, as if the very act of breathing in that space was a challenge to the core of my being. Some way or another everyone had ended up here in an attempt to change a deep-rooted part of ourselves.

I was barely 18.

When my parents decided to send me to Exodus International, I was not asked if I wanted to go. I was told I was going and was signed up shortly thereafter.

About a quarter of the attendees were on the "Xscape Track," composed of all the attendees aged 16–25. The conference consisted of collective speaking segments, as well as breakout sessions irrespective to one's specific track.

The scene around me was haunting. Bewildered eyes darted around the room, eyes glazed with a mix of distress and sincere hope. They seemed to be begging for an escape, not from who they were but from the crushing weight of the "concerned" gazes of loved ones and those around them. It struck me that their misplaced anger was directed inward, instead of back at the outside world where it belonged. A lot of them turned that anger on themselves for not being able to change such an integral part of their being.

The leader of Exodus, Alan Chambers, stole the stage, smiling ear to ear. He used his big grin and enthusiastic stage presence, marked by his theatrical confidence, as he spoke of change, of overcoming, his words laced with a conviction that seemed to feed the crowd's hunger for certainty. He told us that the only thing keeping us from salvation was our inability to control the uncontrollable. But beneath his polished demeanor lay an unsettling dissonance. It was as if he was performing a well-rehearsed play, one that equated salvation with the denial of self.

If Alan Chambers could change his past feelings towards men, surely those in the audience could change too. His message resonated with those present, a group desperate to conform to an imposed standard of normalcy. The air grew heavier with each word, charged with an energy of collective self-reproach. He pushed the idea that our inability to change was a personal failure. He insinuated that it was a deficiency of faith or character, repeating a cruel and dangerous narrative.

The room was filled with people battling themselves, their tears a silent testament to the turmoil wrought by this conflict between identity and doctrine. With each passing moment, the air became thicker with frustration masquerading as positivity. Each speaker presented us with their story of "success" with their own personal "exodus" from a life of what they called sin. Surely, if they could simply change their sexual orientation or gender identity, there must be something wrong with the rest of us who couldn't.

Stories of conversion and redemption were presented as triumphs and celebrated as victories. It was a narrative that glorified self-denial and vilified self-acceptance. They claimed that it was us who were actively inflicting pain and struggle on ourselves. We were said to be the problem. They tried to convince us that we could change but were choosing not to. They insisted that we were the reason for all our pain and suffering. There was never fully a moment of silence, as there was a constant sound of crying in the audience.

When Sy Rogers walked on stage and started talking, I was mesmerized. At the time, I identified as a lesbian, yet I felt an immediate connection to Sy's story. I soaked up every word of his presentation, relating to it in so many ways. I knew from a young age that my soul didn't fit with the body I was given. I didn't have the words to describe the disconnect that I felt around my embodiment. The word *transgender* had been used in such a derogatory way in the environment I grew up in. It had cultivated a fear so deep in my soul that I had never even considered that reality could apply to me.

My heart ripped open hearing Sy describe the hate and judgment that he faced when he identified as a transgender woman. Yet, I couldn't understand why he would trade the freedom he found in his transgender identity for the feeling of so-called safety that religious acceptance offers. I was moved with sympathy for Sy. I felt bad that he was allowing the judgment of others to keep him from unapologetically being himself.

I felt as if I was the only person not sold on the idea that change was possible. I wasn't the only youth forced against my will to attend this event. Yet, it seemed as if I was the only person in the whole conference trying to stand up for myself and others when I could, the only one questioning how much their actions contradicted the fundamentals of what I was taught about Christianity. The principles of love and acceptance that were supposed to underpin our faith were being spun into weapons of the worst kind.

During that very long week, I was repeatedly told I was lost. I was told I was deranged. I was told I was confused. I was told I was the problem. I was told I was sin incarnate, gullible enough to be groomed by these "evil people" who wanted to keep me and others like me from salvation. We were told that *we* were the problems. Our existence was seen as a challenge to be overcome, a deviation from an arbitrary standard of normalcy.

Looking around the room, I could see people were shaking uncontrollably in response to their darkest fears. There were people teetering back and forth on their feet, on the edge of sanity. I could hear the moans and cries. Yet, they all kept fighting to be normal in the eyes of their friends and families, who refused them as they were.

My heart shattered over and over as people tried to console and encourage each other to push through the pain—a pain that was boiling over in each of us. I wonder if each of them is okay and still with us today.

In those moments of shared vulnerability, connections were forged in fleeting whispers and shared glances. I think of Ruth, of Tristian, individuals I met in the briefest of interactions, yet whose stories and struggles were etched into me. We were united in our experience, a small bastion of mutual understanding in a sea of turmoil.

I was there. My feet were stable and sturdy on the ground as I overlooked the auditorium. Yet, my mind was full of "what ifs?" trying to pull me into the same chaotic riptides in which those around me were caught. I held my ground and fought for my sanity. In every breakaway session, I explained how I didn't fit into the boxes they were forcefully trying to put us into. I fought to defend my ability to simply be me.

My experiences, and my understanding of myself, were constantly questioned, dissected, and invalidated by the leaders of the young adult Xscape Track, Julie Rodgers and Ricky Chelette. As a young lesbian, Ricky told me, "Your attraction to women was the product of an absentee mother." I responded that his theory couldn't be further from the truth. As an only child of a single mom, my mother knew the importance of being present for her children and tried her best to be there for me. The box didn't fit.

Ricky then told me, "You must have had an overbearing father who forced masculinity on you." I argued, "This, too, is untrue." I grew up surrounded by brothers, each of us finding our own way in the world. As box after box failed to fit my situation, Julie and Ricky looked for answers that weren't there, seeking any explanation that would fit their narrative.

Boiling with frustration, I felt my heart beating quicker and quicker. I began to reach my breaking point, feeling so unheard and purposefully misunderstood. I vividly recall confronting Julie, saying, "None of these circumstances that you claim cause homosexuality apply to me." She repeated time and again, "One of them has to. Maybe you just need to try harder to remember."

Midway through the week, Julie pulled me out of a group young adult session. She told me, "Ricky and I have determined that you were sexually assaulted as a young child, and you just must not remember." My hands grew clammy and my face cold, and I became faint as the weight of what was just said set in. At a loss for words, I could feel my throat swell as I moved from a state of shock to one of anger. My muscles tensed. I felt stunned, frozen, unable to move. For several moments time stood still. That moment left me reeling from the baselessness and insensitivity of such a suggestion.

Julie coached me in multiple group breakout sessions to get me to remember this sexual trauma that was conveniently fabricated to fit their narrative on homosexuality. Despite the constant gaslighting, I stayed as true to myself as much as I possibly could. I questioned their suggestions with logic: "If I had been sexually assaulted at a young age, wouldn't I have shown other symptoms or signs of trauma?" I asked. "What organizations and medical institutions back the theories you are trying to force on people to convince them that they need to change?" They never listened to me though. Julie would insist, "Plenty of studies have shown evidence that people can change." However, she could never name them, nor could Ricky. They would argue, "It isn't your place to question the Lord."

Ricky and Julie decided that the only option for me was for

them to attempt to force me to recall the story they had just fabricated. I was told by both of them, "You must try your hardest to remember the sexual traumas in order to free yourself from the burden they bring." If I couldn't, I was informed that the future of my soul would be eternal damnation.

I caught myself glancing over my shoulders more, increasingly cognizant of what I said and around whom. I began to realize again just how alone I was in those moments.

Julie repeated constantly, "Change is possible, and I am proof of it." Exodus preached, "Anyone who doesn't change isn't trying hard enough because it is possible for everyone." Julie recommended a variety of ways to respond to any of the temptations we may have felt. She said, "Burning yourself by heating up a quarter with a lighter and pressing into your skin is an easy way to correct yourself after impure thoughts." She went so far as to suggest that ankles and feet were a discreet location to do it.

The days of the conference were long, each moment stretching into an eternity of second-guessing and furrowed brows. Nights were restless, filled with pacing and a desperate search for any remaining sense of reality. The peer-pressure to conform, to accept and embody the narrative, was almost unbearable. I was drowning, gasping for breaths of truth amid the tides of lies. Each night, I walked back and forth in the empty halls of the college dorm, trying to ground myself while fighting off the pressure of altering myself to meet the needs of those who refused to accept me.

I couldn't sleep. I could barely eat. It was hard to stomach anything, even the vagueness of passing conversation. I became reclusive and couldn't trust anyone. I came with a conversion-therapy young-adults group from Texas. However, I was aware that I was one of the only ones who was not on board with what we were being told.

I knew, deep down, that my feelings were innate, that the love I felt was as real and valid as any other. The God I had been taught to believe in, the one who was supposed to know and love me as I was, seemed distant in the face of the conference message. It was a stark contradiction of the belief that we were all made in God's image, that each of us, in all our diversity, is a reflection of the divine.

If there was a hell, I was living it that week.

As the conference drew to a close, a crescendo of fervent speeches and emotional testimonies filled the air. People spoke of their struggles and their journeys toward an imposed ideal of normalcy. I could hear their voices quiver with fear and see their faces still painted in shame. It was painful to see the false hope cultivated in people who desperately wanted to feel more at peace with themselves.

On the final day, I stood at the back of the auditorium, my heart heavy with a mix of relief and sadness. I breathed in deeply with relief that this ordeal was almost over. My cheeks stained with streams of sadness, overflowing for those who left believing they were less than worthy in their natural state. The final speaker took the stage, their words a familiar echo of the sentiments expressed throughout the week. But by then, I was no longer listening.

My thoughts turned inward, reflecting on my journey. I thought about my family, my friends, and the life that awaited me outside this place. I realized that this experience, as painful as it was, had solidified something within me. A deep, unshakable conviction in my identity, a resolve to live authentically despite the pressures to conform.

As I walked out of the auditorium for the last time, the cool evening air hit me like a balm. The sky was now a deep indigo, dotted with stars, a vast canvas that reminded me of the endless possibilities that lay ahead.

The Exodus International Freedom Conference, in all its attempts to suppress and change, had inadvertently given me a gift: understanding who I am and, just as importantly, who I am not.

# Chapter 14

# BEHIND CLOSET DOORS

## COLIN BLAND

I remember walking down the corridor to B's office, my heart racing. This was my second therapy session with B, a licensed professional counselor in downtown Columbia, South Carolina. I had managed to stave off any serious conversations the week before in our first session while B and I broke the ice with small talk over a game of checkers. I was hurting, and I was told I could be helped, but every time I tried to identify the hurt out loud, I choked on the words. There was a part of me that seemed certain that some secrets were better kept unspoken, and each time I tried to share mine, another part of my body would steal the air out of my lungs. As B opened the door to his office, my whole body recoiled, and I intuitively knew something about this week was going to be different.

I walked through the door and sat down on the client couch directly across from the door. I wore a sweatshirt this week because the week before I left with irritated skin from B's burlap couch. He asked me if I would like a Coke—I responded with an enthusiastic *yes*, thinking it would buy me a few moments alone to calm down. I tried to steady myself with deep breaths while B ventured down the hall. I inhaled deeply and held my breath to slow my heart, but the moment I exhaled the rapid thumping returned with a vengeance, beating against my ribcage. I squirmed in unease when the cracked door was pushed open, and I was even more disappointed when B emerged with a Pepsi.

B closed the door to his office behind him and handed me the Pepsi as he sat down in his armchair across from me. B's office was uncomfortably small; there were no windows, and the room was barely large enough for the burlap loveseat and his oversized armchair. This was one of the few times I was relieved I wasn't any taller. Being under 5'6" saved me from navigating an uncomfortable game of footsies with B as he sat opposite from me in his armchair.

B started our session with simple small talk before trying to ease us into the reasons I was pursuing therapy. He inquired about mundane topics, ranging from how my week was going to what I had done over the weekend. Before long, there wasn't anything trivial left to delay the inevitable, and B pivoted to the elephant in the room.

"As much as I like playing checkers, we both know that's not why you're here," B started. He wasn't a tall man, and he was a little stockier, but he did have a soft expression as he was speaking. "Do you think you're comfortable to start unpacking what's going on?"

"Yeah..." I exhaled quickly. We both paused for a moment as I was trying to dig deep to find words and make sounds. "I don't feel like I'm who I'm supposed to be... I feel like everyone wants me to be perfect, but I feel… broken? Everyone wants me to be normal, but I'm not…" I swallowed hard. I couldn't bring myself to say the phrase, "I'm gay," out loud so I improvised. "I like boys instead of girls."

B gently leaned back in his armchair without changing his expression. He made eye contact with me and gestured to his face. "You see my expression?" I nodded. "What you said doesn't scare me." I breathed a slight sigh of relief as he continued. "I've heard things like this from people before, and I'll tell you the same thing I told them. It's okay to not be okay—it's just not okay to stay that way."

B offered a warm smile, and I began to buy wholesale into what he was saying. I felt like the hard part was over. I had finally told someone what felt like my dirtiest secret, and this person was positioned to help me. After all, that's what he was getting paid for, right?

"I have some questions for you to help me understand what's going on." B got his legal pad ready to take some notes. "In my experience, people like you have just gotten some wires crossed in the wrong places in the brain. This can happen for all sorts of reasons, and I want to try to understand where your wires may have gotten crossed." B paused and looked down at his notepad and scribbled something down before he continued. "Were you ever sexually abused?"

I was taken aback. If this is what caused other people's same-sex attraction, what did it say about me if I hadn't been sexually abused? I sat for a few moments with the question, trying to unpack its implications before I finally gave my one-word answer: "No."

"Are you sure?" B quipped back without hesitation. In that moment, I wasn't sure anymore. Had I just forgotten, and that's what made me gay? Who abused me? How old was I if this happened? I mulled this over again for a few more moments before I told him that, yes, I was sure. This prompted another series of uncomfortable questions trying to pin the blame of my same-sex attractions on something tangible. Have you ever seen gay porn? Do you masturbate? Do you read any gay books? Do you watch TV shows with gay characters? What are your relationships like with your parents? Before long, B found his smoking gun, and we were able to diagnose the catalyst for my homosexuality.

"You have a good relationship with your parents, but you said your dad was in the military?" B had been furiously taking notes as he bombarded me with questions.

"Yes, my dad served an active-duty tour for a year in Iraq when I was in third and fourth grade, and he was gone again in another state when I started middle school." I looked down at my hands. I had them folded neatly in my lap to conceal their trembling while my brain was working overtime. I was making the connections in real time, just as B was. Of course, my father being gone had made me this way.

"I suspected there was something that caused this." B paused. "Have you discussed this at all with your parents?" I shook my head. "Why? Are you afraid they will think you did something to your brother?" I completely froze. My face recoiled in disgust at the suggestion, but I also retreated inward at the insinuation I would harm my family in such a heinous way. It became even more clear to me I had to change. I didn't want to be perceived as a predator.

"No, I would never do that. I just don't want to hurt like this anymore." My eyes began stinging as they welled up with salty tears. My stomach rose into my throat as if I was on a roller-coaster, feeling also as if I had swallowed a brick. I could barely pull in enough air to finish my thought. "I just want it to stop. I'm so confused, and I think about this all the time, and I just want that voice in my head that keeps saying, 'I'm still here,' to go away." I buried my face in my hands and wiped the dampness from my eyes.

"Is this voice an audible voice?" B inquired. I didn't like his question. I was afraid, knowing he was a Christian, that he would suggest I needed an exorcism.

"No, no, it's not like that," I protested, "It's… just this feeling, and I always know it's there."

"We can fix this," B assured me. "Remember, it's okay to not be okay. We just don't want to stay that way." He gave another soft smile of affirmation. "So, have you ever heard of Pavlov?" I shook my head. He proceeded to fill me in. "Pavlov did an experiment where he fed his dogs juicy steak every time he rang a specific bell. After doing this for a while, the dogs associated that bell with eating meat. This is the same thing that's happened with you. You experience good and healthy desires for the wrong thing. We just need to get those wires uncrossed, and you'll start to feel those healthy feelings for girls."

B proceeded to give me instructions on how I could retrain myself like Pavlov's dogs. I needed to be hypervigilant about making sure I didn't permit myself to let my eyes linger on men. I needed to, instead, focus on women. B instructed me on how to objectify women. My homework was to look at young women and enjoy their breasts and butts. I needed to focus on their curves and imagine what they felt like and thank God that we were given such beauty in the female form. I was uncomfortable at the proposition; I had a younger sister after all, and I didn't want other guys looking at her like that. B assured me that this wasn't anything like lusting—it was just being thankful.

Alternatively, whenever I was tempted to think about a cute guy or stare for a second too long, B told me I needed to think of the nastiest images possible. We fabricated a scenario where I saw a cute guy in some ambiguous public space, and B asked me what I was thinking of. The only things that came to mind were vomit and trash. B celebrated the negative association and said that over time I'd retrain myself, just like Pavlov's dogs. He assured me that I would eventually associate only negative feelings with homosexual attractions and only positive feelings toward women.

B also gave me some other suggestions on ways to "uncross my wires." He indicated that my masculinity needed some reinforcing since my dad wasn't present for part of my early childhood. I needed to have "healthy" relationships with other guys around my age by doing traditionally masculine activities like sports and video games. B also suggested down the road that I hire a speech therapist to help reshape the way I talked. He didn't like how my "tongue curled femininely" when I spoke. He said the way I talked could betray me, and gay men would undoubtedly make advances on me because of how I spoke. Until I could hire someone, it would be worthwhile practicing how to say no to homosexual advances. We spent the remainder of the session practicing saying, "No," to the promiscuous gay men supposedly lurking around every corner. We role played, and my line was "I'm not sure what's going on here, but I don't want to be a part of it."

I had just started high school when I met B in our first session. I had heard negative messages about gay people for years from my youth group and school, where off-color jokes were made with gay people as the punchline. My chronic acne was already enough ammunition for uncomfortable comments about my appearance, and I knew I didn't want to add fuel to the fire with speculations about my sexuality. I wasn't equipped with the language to explain how I was feeling, and I certainly didn't believe I could ever be happy being openly gay. For years, I'd heard negative sentiments about gay men in particular. They were responsible for the AIDS epidemic, and they were the primary indication of a society's collapse; look at the fall of Rome, and there you'll see the homosexuals. I knew what being gay meant to the Southerners around me, and I knew that I didn't want that. I believed B could help me change.

And terrifyingly, so did he.

# Chapter 15

# CONVERT

## GEMMA HICKEY

I was 15 the first time I had sex with a girl.

"I dare you to touch my stomach, Gemma," she whispered playfully.

When I took her up on it, she told me not to stop there.

I had no idea where the encounter would lead, but that didn't matter. Driven by instinct, my hands traveled her curves like a winding road. The heat from her body ignited a fire within me. When I took her into my mouth, the person I pretended to be was extinguished. I could no longer hide from who I was, and it would take years to rise from the ashes.

I grew up in St. John's, on the east coast of Newfoundland and Labrador. The island was visited and claimed, or rather stolen, from the Beothuk, its first inhabitants before establishment took place by settlers in the early 17th century. Currently, people of all nationalities call St. John's home, but many, my family included, trace their roots back to Irish settlers, shaping my upbringing within the Irish Catholic tradition. At baptism, when the priest traced an invisible cross on my tiny forehead, I was branded in body, mind, and spirit. At that moment, my innate sin was cleansed, and my so-called education began. The influence of the church's teachings infiltrated every aspect of my life, spanning from my home and school to the broader fabric of society.

I was assigned female at birth, and throughout my child-hood, my designated gender posed as an obstacle to pursuing what I truly desired. Participating in sports was discouraged as a girl. Wearing dresses felt foreign, I couldn't relate to them, and they attracted unwanted attention from the older boys in my neighborhood. I tried to conform, but inhabiting my own body felt foreign, as if I were a stranger in a strange land. I knew I was unique but had no language to describe what I was thinking and feeling and no one to compare myself to. The era was vastly different, and acceptance was scarce. Not only did I live on an island, but I also felt like one, isolated and alone. I was taught to believe that gay and lesbian people were child molesters and unfit parents and that transgender people were predominantly involved in sex work. These erroneous stereotypes prevailed, despite the declassification of homosexuality as a mental illness three years prior to my birth. It's no wonder I felt as if there was something wrong with me when I developed feelings for a girl. Whenever she entered my mind, I took cold showers or listened to loud heavy metal. I even started having sex with my boyfriend. All attempts at fixing myself failed, however, and so I went to see my family doctor to ask him for help. He referred me to a therapist in the next office, and it almost cost me my life.

In the reception area, a mix of nervousness and uncertainty came over me while I waited for my name to be called. With my body's fight-or-flight response in full swing, my eyes were fixed on the exit sign above the door. Small beads of sweat clung to my skin like dew on grass. The rhythmic tap of the receptionist's fingers on the keyboard echoed like a downpour in the corner, intensifying my fear. Just as I contemplated leaving, an older woman appeared, inviting me into one of the offices. Her jet-black hair, threaded with delicate strands of grey resembling drifting ash, cascaded over the frames of her dark-rimmed glasses. Around her neck hung a sizable wooden crucifix. Unsure of what lay ahead, I trusted my doctor and followed her lead.

The room held a small round table at its center, its arrangement purposeful, positioning two seats to face each other. On the table, the leaves of a potted plant curled like fingers, hovering above a box of tissues as if attempting to reach for one. Even with the walls adorned in a soft off-white hue and the window flooding the space with sunlight, I found myself suffocating within the confines of the room. After a few sessions, I sensed that the only means of finding relief was to openly confess the secret buried deep within me, so I blurted it out. She comforted me by affirming to me that her intervention, guided by faith in God, would free me from the weight of carrying this heavy burden. I was eager to believe her, especially since the absence of support had made the situation unbearable.

Over the course of the year, I attended regular sessions where she consistently asserted that my attraction to girls was rooted in a desire to imitate them. Despite my insistence that I never identified as a girl, she urged me to place my trust in God and focus on prayer. She attributed my "confusion" around sexual orientation and gender identity to family dysfunction and child-hood trauma, assigning me readings reinforcing heterosexuality and traditional gender roles as homework. During each session, I was required to summarize the content in my own words, and she frequently linked being in a same-sex relationship with going to hell. We would end by praying the Lord's Prayer together.

At home, my nerves heightened as I had to conceal the reading materials from my parents. Every night, I prayed fervently, working myself into such intensity that it brought on a sweat each time. Often, I'd find myself in tears, curled up in the fetal position on my bed, her remarks turning like a revolving door in my head, until sleep rescued me. Despite numerous sessions, my feelings for the girl remained unchanged. Despair followed me like a lingering shadow. The passage of days and nights became a seamless blur, rendering the concept of time inconsequential. School became an arduous task, a relentless chore amid an overwhelming fog of hopelessness. Believing death to be my sole escape, I grappled with the realization that both suicide and homosexuality were considered sins. Deciding that ending my life was a preferable alternative to the hell I was living, I stopped praying and wrote a goodbye poem to my parents.

Dear Mom and Dad,
Please don't be mad
I'm gay
Was I born this way?
It's a sin
In our religion
And since birth
A hell on earth
All the lies

A thin disguise
I can hide no more
Fight a secret war
They have won
It is done.

※

It was a crisp fall day in Ottawa on November 29, 2021. Canada's capital was bustling as usual. On the sidewalk, people passed one another like cars traveling on a two-lane highway. I was headed on foot toward the office of David Lametti, the then Minister of Justice and Attorney General of Canada. The federal government was moving forward with their campaign promise to ban conversion therapy, and as a widely known activist, I had been invited to speak alongside the minister at the press conference. I couldn't sit in the House of Commons due to the pandemic, but the minister's staff arranged for me to watch from a television screen in his office. Together, we stood arm-in-arm as we witnessed the House erupt into a spectacle of applause and cross-party embraces—a miraculously rare occurrence of bi-partisan cooperation. Conservative justice critic Rob Moore presented a motion to fast-track Bill C-4, an act to amend the criminal code making conversion therapy illegal in Canada, and Members of Parliament unanimously adopted it. No MP spoke out against it. The legislation would proceed to the Senate. What a day to be alive, I thought to myself. My life had come full circle.

We moved quickly between buildings on our way to the press conference. The Gothic-Revival style architecture of the Victorian era was evident at every turn. I was brought to a large foyer outside where the press conference was taking place. Ministers David Lametti, Marci Ien, Randy Boissonnault, Pascale St-Onge, and MP Rob Oliphant joined us shortly after we arrived. We were all feeling joyful as we posed for pictures. Before an aide informed us it was time to start, Ministers Boissonnault, St-Onge, and I noted how significant this day was.

We entered the room following the prearranged order. Minister Lametti was the first to enter, followed by me, then Ministers Ien and Boissonnault, and, finally, MP Oliphant. A line of Canadian flags stood at attention when we made our entrance onto the stage while reporters remained seated, their chairs strategically placed on the checkerboard carpet like pawns in a chess game. When we took our seats, the interpreter, positioned at the far end of the stage, provided an overview of the press conference and invited Minister Lametti to give opening remarks. Following the Land Acknowledgment, the minister gave a resolute statement on the importance of banning conversion therapy before introducing me. Suddenly, it was my turn to speak. I removed my mask, cleared my throat, and began to speak.

## Speaking notes at the Bill C-4 press conference, November 29, 2021

G. Hickey

*I was 15 years old when I confessed to my family doctor that I had a crush on a girl. I thought I was sick. I remember shaking in his office. A mere shadow of the person you see before you today. Back then, I identified as female because I was assigned that gender at birth. I* was raised Roman Catholic, and my church taught that being homosexual or transgender was wrong. Society reinforced these beliefs. My doctor referred me to the therapist in the next office.

When she greeted me at the door my eyes gravitated towards the large wooden crucifix that hung around her neck on the outside of her blouse.

"Welcome, Gemma," the therapist said. "You're safe here."

She lied.

After a few sessions, I told her that I thought I was gay.

"Don't worry," she assured me in a soft voice. "We can fix that."

She told me that homosexuality is a premature sexuality, that when I became heterosexual, I would reach full maturity as a human being. According to her, my feelings for girls were rooted in the desire to be like them. When I told her I always wanted to be like a boy, she added that if I prayed hard enough, God would make me better. She prescribed me anti-depressants in the meantime.

After months of therapy, I still felt the same, so I decided to end my life. At a party one night, I swallowed all the pills in the medicine cabinet and washed them down with a flask of rum. My friends found me passed out on the floor, and I was rushed to the hospital. I spent the beginning of my high school senior year on a psychiatric ward but was sent home once I met with the psychiatrist. When he told me that there was nothing wrong with me, his words were like medicine to my soul. As I left the hospital, I vowed to do whatever I could to ensure that young people did not feel as I did. The activist in me was born.

I devoted the next three decades of my life to LGBTQ2S+ advocacy, co-leading movements that fostered societal recognition, such as same-sex marriage, adoption, and gender-neutral identification, among others, because no one believed me when I told them that conversion therapy still existed.

Conversion therapy is the pseudo-medical practice of attempting to change a person's sexual orientation and gender identity to heterosexual or cisgender. Misleading marketing campaigns have promoted this view for years, enabling countless vulnerable youth to be placed in harm's way. According to the United Nations, the perpetuation of this so-called therapy is a human rights catastrophe, yet it still happens all over the world. Efforts to restrict and ban the practice have recently gained momentum due to the hard work of survivors like myself, who have shared our stories in the hopes that others will be spared. Sadly, many lives still end tragically by suicide.

Finally at 45 years of age I can say that I'm the best version of myself. I'm proud to be transgender, proud to be a Newfoundlander and Labradorian, and proud to live in a country where conversion therapy is banned. I want to thank the government for following through on their promise. Conversion therapy is homophobic and transphobic and doesn't belong in Canada or anywhere else.

To young people everywhere, you can beat the statistics as well as the odds, just like I did. You have a fundamental human right to be who you are. And once you learn how to love yourself, the rest is history. Take it from me.

And to the ones who have not lived to see this day, we honour your memory today and every day.

Thank you.

On December 14, 2017, following a triumphant legal victory

against the provincial government, I became the proud holder of the country's first gender-neutral birth certificate. It felt like a reclamation of self, a sort of rebirth. The sensation of holding it in my hand for the first time was indescribable. Tracing the X with my fingers felt like a test, almost as if I anticipated it to vanish.

"We won't be erased," I thought to myself, feeling a sense of permanence.

Armed with my updated birth certificate, I immediately launched a campaign to push the federal government for a gender-neutral passport, which I obtained not long after. My new passport has done more than just allow me entry into other countries; it has also paved the way for others, opening gates that were once closed.

A second chance at life is a rare gift. Embracing it whole-heartedly, I've let go of the pointless ritual of worrying about others' judgments, and the era of attempting to conform to a predetermined mold is safely behind me. Breaking away from the path set out for me by the church, I've carved my own way and become a convert in the truest sense.

# Chapter 16

# SETTING CAPTIVES FREE

## TYLER KRUMLAND

I'd like to think that I'm a brave person, someone who will stand his ground. But everyone has their limits, and I am no exception. When I begin to feel unsafe, a sharp chill runs down my spine causing the hair on my arms to stand up. I become hyper-aware of everything around me, making sure I know where my exit is. My throat tightens, and it seems as if each breath I take in goes down with a quiver. This is often the feeling I get when I'm around most evangelical churches. But it wasn't always that way. At one point, the church was a place that felt like a refuge. However, that was all before I had spent years trying to change a part of me they taught me was wrong, a part of me that never needed changing.

I was 26 and finishing the second year of my youth ministry internship at the church where I grew up. I was preparing to enter seminary in the fall to continue studying toward one day being a full-time pastor. I always saw entering the pastorate as a calling that shouldn't be taken lightly, striving to do whatever I could to be the best version of myself. My faith was the most important thing to me and something I thought about constantly; I was always searching for ways to go deeper. I wanted to be someone to whom the students I served looked up. This meant I spent a lot of time reflecting, praying, and journaling.

Though I felt most of my life was blemish free, there was one thing about me I dared not speak about, a secret that I vowed to never share out of fear of the rejection I would receive from everyone around me. I couldn't even say the words: "I am gay." Well, I guess at that point I would have said I struggled with *same-sex attraction* because I had never pursued a "gay lifestyle," so I wouldn't have called myself gay. But of all the things in my life that needed to be eradicated, this was at the top of my list.

The program I was a part of wasn't likely what most would picture when they hear the words *conversion therapy*. No, this wasn't a secret camp to which I was whisked away to in the middle of the night against my will but rather an online program I willingly signed myself up for that described itself as a "60-day interactive course that would teach me to enjoy a newfound relationship with the Lord and how to find freedom from homosexuality." It seemed like the logical choice since I believed I needed to be straight and to have this part of me put to death in order to follow God with my whole heart.

The concept was simple. Each day when I signed into my account, I would be presented with a short Bible-study lesson. These lessons included a small chunk of scripture, followed by some reflection questions around the lesson for me to answer. Typically, these questions were written in a way that had me compare what was happening in the Bible story to my struggle with *sexual temptations*, as they called it. When I signed up, I was also assigned a mentor, someone who had been through the course himself and graduated.

After each lesson, I was required to answer three questions: 1) Did I notice myself attracted to someone of the same sex today? 2) Did I indulge in pornography? 3) Did I give into any form of self-gratification around my desires? Once I answered these questions and completed my lesson, I would click send, and it would go to my mentor who would review my answers and then send me a message with feedback.

At first, my mentor, Mark, seemed fine. He would send me a pretty direct and brief response after each of my lessons, but he always seemed a bit removed and cold. He never really asked me how I was doing. I really wanted to find freedom, so I was always honest when answering the final three questions, particularly admitting that I was still noticing attraction to other men. If I wasn't honest, then how would I expect to find freedom?

I had thought someone who had been where I was would have been kind, understanding, and sympathetic, but that was not the case. Each time I told him that I was still attracted to other men, he would berate me with scripture and cruel feedback. He reminded me that 1 Corinthians 6:9–10 says, "'Do you not know that the unrighteous will not inherit the kingdom of God? Do not be deceived; neither the sexually immoral, nor idolaters, nor adulterers, nor men who practice homosexuality will inherit the Kingdom of God." "Do you not want to inherit the Kingdom of God, Tyler? Do you not want to be in eternity with all your family and friends? That's what's going to happen unless you turn things around and show that you truly love God like you claim you do."

At that point in my life, becoming straight was the one thing I was made to believe I wanted most. It was more than a want, according to the church; it was a necessity for my very soul. I poured my time and heart into each of those lessons, and nobody was more disappointed than I was that I wasn't seeing the changes promised in this course. So, when Mark would come at me, telling me that I was being unserious and apathetic about my lessons, he was essentially telling me in so many words that I was a failure. His words confirmed that those awful things I had believed about myself were true. Not only was I letting myself down, but I was a disappointment to the God I had committed my life to.

The only help Mark would ever offer me was to tell me to pray more and not go into places like the gym where I would see other men who could cause me to "stumble" as he put it. He gave me tips for success like wearing a rubber band around my wrist that I would snap when I found myself attracted to another guy. He told me that the sting of the rubber band would reorient my mind to not allow those evil feelings to persist. He encouraged me to read scripture about what happens to the sexually depraved who don't repent and remind myself that if I didn't change, that was my future. He told me that each time I completed these lessons but he didn't see change, I was wasting his time and God's.

If there is one thing that has always been true about me it is that I'm a pathological people-pleaser, so to tell me I was wasting not only his time but also God's ruined me. I was doing everything I could to take it seriously, not to mention I was so closeted that I couldn't process what I was going through with anybody else. I was making sure to do my lessons first thing each morning. I had taken his advice and printed off tons of Bible verses that I had taped all around the mirror in my bathroom and I would memorize them and meditate on them throughout my day. I would recite the Lord's Prayer over and over when I was feeling "tempted." I prayed constantly, and I started to avoid places that he told me were not good for me. When we sang worship songs in church, I would do as the lessons encouraged and think about how I was lucky that God still loved me even though I believed that my existence would be seen as a mistake by those around me or something broken beyond repair until I had this under control. Yet, regardless, my attraction to men continued. The more often I noticed it the more I would find my confidence in myself and my ability to reach this goal crumbling right before me. I found myself obsessively worrying that the rest of my life would be spent fighting against myself.

I was irritable and on edge, easily set off by any minor inconvenience. I'd be in line at the grocery store and the person in front of me would be moving too slowly, causing me to sigh in frustration at the extra two minutes added to my errand while also causing my blood pressure to rise. I had a hard time relaxing, and it made falling asleep an impossible task as my mind wandered to the darkest potential outcomes for my story if I ultimately failed at becoming straight. I assumed I was feeling this way because of my failure to succeed in these courses, as Mark continuously told me. These things were the fruit I was bearing because of who I was at my core.

Twenty days into the course, I received one of the worst messages from Mark. He told me that he was done working with me because he didn't believe I was taking any of it seriously. If I truly wanted to change, then I needed to get my act together and finally make the efforts he didn't believe I was making. He felt it was best that I take a break from the course and sit with my thoughts and when I was serious about things, I could start the program over. He said that if I stayed on the track I was on, where I was still attracted to other men, I was destined for an eternity in Hell.

In that moment, those dark fears that kept me awake at night seemed as if they were certain to be my future. I was so hopeful when I first found this program, picturing a future of being married to a woman while working as a pastor, where being gay was just a bad memory from my past. Reading the testimonies of the people who had already gone through the course and hearing about their success inspired me. I truly thought it would offer me the freedom I had been hoping for. The program was called Setting Captives Free, but I still felt shackled by this part of me, and the person who was supposed to help and encourage me only made me feel worse. I believed the things he said about and to me. I had failed, but I couldn't tell anyone because in doing so, I would not only expose this failure but also out myself. I had nowhere to go except inward. So, like so many things in my past I stuffed it deep down inside me and stepped back from the program. I reflected in my journals, writing about how broken and lost I felt with little hope that things could ever turn around for me.

About four months later, I mustered up the courage to

attempt the course one more time. Though I did it again and had a much kinder mentor this time, I never finished. I made it to the final lesson, which asked me to write my testimony of how I had been freed from homosexuality, but I couldn't bring myself to do it. I couldn't lie. I wouldn't lie.

I did a quick search of the program recently and found that it has since been discontinued, with the pastor who started it issuing an apology statement.

I don't believe he was sorry for what he did, just how he did it.

I tried to read it, but similar to my attempts to make my way through the program, I couldn't finish it. The difference was, this time, it was my choice not to finish. Evangelical pastors who did not affirm the queer community had been given more of my time and heart than they ever deserved, and no empty platitude this pastor could offer would undo the damage that had been done. I decided in that moment I wasn't going to waste another moment thinking about setting captives free. I had too much life yet to be lived.

# Chapter 17

# GAY CHRISTIAN SPEED DATING

### LUCAS F. W. WILSON

"What do you think the guys in the group are going to be like?" I asked as I pushed my tray forward and took the last bite of my supper.

"I'm honestly so curious to find out," Thad said, his cat eyes glinting. He sat back in his chair and lifted his veiny arms behind his head. His dark armpit hair peeked out from under his t-shirt. I couldn't stop staring. *Was he wearing deodorant?* I wondered. All I wanted to do was stick my nose in his pits, inhale, and inhale deeply.

Thad and I were sitting in Liberty's cafeteria. Liberty University—the evangelical college that touted itself as "the world's most exciting university"—was where we had both chosen to study, and, like our peers, we wanted to receive a Christian education in order to, up on graduation, set the world on fire for Jesus.

It was the second or third time Thad and I had hung out. We had met when Steph, the gal I was half-heartedly trying to "pursue" at the time, suggested he and I connect. When I told

Steph I was more attracted to guys than women, to my surprise, she didn't hightail it. Instead, she thought I could speak with her friend Thad, someone who also struggled with same-sex attraction and who, she said, could potentially help me figure out my desire for men. When she had first told me about him, I secretly hoped he would be handsome. Even though I believed I wanted to become straight—not to mention sexually pure—my hormones were nevertheless raging. So, when Thad and I eventually met up, I was delighted to find out that he was, in fact, a major babe.

Thad was one of the few guys like me I knew personally on campus. With the exception of one friend I had met early on in my time at Liberty, there were only a couple of others I had gotten to know who also dealt with same-sex attraction. One was a Spiritual Life Director on my freshman dorm, with whom I had an incredibly bizarre one-night stand and who stopped talking to me immediately thereafter.

It was because of my short tryst with my Spiritual Life Director that I initially went to meet with Pastor Dane Emerick, the man on campus who promised to help male students who were struggling with same-sex attraction and the man who was leading the group Thad and I were to attend that evening. At the time I hooked up with my Spiritual Life Director, I felt that I had no one else to speak with at a university that fined, punished, and even expelled students for acting on their same-sex attractions.

So, when Steph introduced Thad and me, I was relieved to meet someone else who shared my struggle. But the flesh was weak, and I could only hope that it was for him, too.

Thad, however, was in no way interested. He talked to me as

if I were his younger brother. Even though I was always down for some good old-fashioned role play, it was clear that Thad was not—at least not with me.

"I have a feeling I already know who most of the guys are who're going to be there tonight," I said.

We were waiting out the clock until it was time to head over to the group meeting not far from the cafeteria. The group was for those at Liberty who were like us, those whose eyes quietly met the eyes of other guys when no one else was looking, those who also surveyed the sea of deliciously skimpy tank tops in the gym that exposed slick backs and sweaty pecs—that is to say, those who liked cock.

Both Thad and I had met one-on-one with Pastor Dane for years. But after we agreed we wanted to have some intel into who else dealt with same-sex attraction on campus, we both asked if we could join the group—especially since, as each of us argued, we had been making so much progress toward becoming sexually pure. Pastor Dane agreed.

"Same," Thad replied. "And I'm not overly excited about those guys to be honest—none have caught my eye."

On Liberty's campus, there were the usual suspects who covertly signaled that they were of the persuasion, telling us their secret on the daily without ever having to say a word. Some were cute enough, but similar to Thad, I wasn't really interested.

Thad continued: "But maybe there'll be some surprises."

I liked hanging out with Thad because although he was trying to fight his same-sex desires most of the time, he was also a fellow naughty boy—one who occupied both the Liberty bubble and "the world." He was realistic about his and my situation of being attracted to men—but, sometimes, he was almost too realistic. He told me that after graduation, he planned to head out west to California and finally figure out if God really said it's not okay to be gay. Even though I wanted to do the same when I moved home to Toronto, the prospect also terrified me. I constantly wondered, *What happens if I'm wrong?* I didn't want to give up my relationship to God, and I certainly didn't want to go to hell. So, I remained within the fold and by and large followed the straight and narrow, despite the occasional late-night evening in my dorm room with a jar of Vaseline and tissues, perusing the French websites I knew that were undetected by Liberty's anti-porn blocker.

"Let us pray," I responded wryly.

After grabbing our knapsacks and returning our trays, we left the cafeteria and made our way over to the Music Hall, where our meeting was to be held. Though many Liberty students knew that the group existed, no one on campus—other than its members—knew where or when Pastor Dane's group meetings were held. We were a secret. As we walked over, the cover of night offered us a sense of anonymity. But regardless of the darkness and despite how no one knew where we were headed, I nonetheless felt as if I was being watched—something I felt regularly on campus. I was paranoid that I was going to bump into someone I knew and, without an alibi, would have to explain where I was going. Thankfully, we walked the hundred or so meters and entered the building unseen.

As we meandered through the halls, we finally found ourselves outside the meeting room door. My heart continued to race, no longer out of nagging anxiety of being seen but instead out of eager anticipation of who was on the other side of the wall.

I turned and smiled at Thad, and we stepped inside, one after the other. In front of us was a group of guys, buzzing and chattering. They paused their conversations, turned, and looked us up and down, taking us in. Slowly, they resumed talking with one another, but they kept looking back at us. As we walked further into the room, I could feel their not-so-furtive gaze still on us. I scanned the dimly lit scene in front of me. Thad and I were right: It was mostly the guys on campus we thought would be there. But as I took in the company I would be keeping for the next hour, I saw him.

He was sitting on the floor, next to a couch, staring straight back at me. This was not new for him and me, as I had seen him on campus constantly, and when our eyes had inevitably met, they lingered just a *little* too long. I had always wondered if he, too, struggled with what I struggled with. Seeing him in this meeting, however, seemed to finally clear things up. In my head, I had called him Phil because he looked like Phil Diffy from Disney's *Phil of the Future*. Now was my chance to introduce myself.

I turned and looked at Thad who was behind me, and he flashed his teeth in a wide grin as if to say, *We're actually here, huh?* I gestured for us to go sit down on the couch. As a few attendees stepped aside as we approached our destination, I suddenly saw someone I had known through a friend. He and I were only really acquaintances, but he was on the couch, next to my crush, which gave me a good excuse as to why I was hurriedly beelining it in his direction.

"Oh, hey!" I said.

"Oh, hey, Luke! How are ya?" my acquaintance responded in somewhat of an enthused but unsurprised reply. I wondered if our mutual friend had told him about me.

He stood up, gave me a hug, and pointed next to the couch and said, "This is my friend Mac."

I looked down at Mac who was still sitting on the floor—his eyes at the same level as my crotch—and smiled. "Hi, Mac. I'm Luke."

Mac smiled nervously and greeted me back. It felt as if he recognized me, too. I introduced Thad to them both, and the three of us who were standing sat down on the couch, pressed tight against one another, close to Mac on the ground. We chit chatted for a few minutes before leaning back to observe the guys who stood talking to each other in front of us.

"Hey, *man!*" one of them said to another.

"What's up, *dude?*" the other responded.

"*Bro*, not much! Just living the dream!"

I sat there listening, red-faced and cringing. It sounded as if they were trying to approximate the discourse of some gay locker-room porno. I was by no means the epitome of masculinity, but I also never spoke in a way that felt this inauthentic. I consistently tried as best I could to speak and act like the man God intended me to be—which Pastor Dane had instructed me to do, if I wanted to find attraction to the opposite sex—but I refused to talk like *this*. I knew why the guys in this room were acting as they were—they were just following Dane's directives. But even for someone who performed on a daily basis like me, the room stunk of artifice.

Pastor Dane soon began the meeting with the assistance of a

student who appeared to be his sidekick for the night. They led us through prayer, scripture, and an open discussion of our shared struggle, that which had brought us together. We talked about what it meant to be a man, God's man, and what went wrong for those of us who did not live up to that standard. We shared strategies of how to fight temptations, how to resist Satan's advances, and how to become both godly and sexually pure. Pastor Dane reminded us that if we were to live more fully in the world of men, we could eventually find a woman to marry and lead complete, happy lives. These promises fueled me. They offered me hope for a better future, one that would finally allow me to be like my guy friends who were dating women and getting engaged.

"Doing the things that men do allows us to become the men God calls us to be. That's why, in part, we've planned to go on a hike this weekend—to get sweaty! To get into nature! And to just be *men* together!" Pastor Dane said excitedly. "Who in here's coming with?"

Several guys lifted their hands.

*No chance in hell,* I thought. As much as I had wanted to meet other guys like me on campus, it became quickly and painfully clear as we stepped foot in this meeting that these were not the guys I wanted to hang out with. There had to be others like me on campus, those I'd rather get hot and sweaty with and who wanted the same. Like, for instance, Mac.

We broke out into small groups to discuss what Pastor Dane had shared with us. His lesson was not novel, as it was the same script that he had presented to me in our one-on-one meetings—and I assumed it was the same he had proffered to the others in theirs. I was thankful for the repetition that defined his messages—his consistency was comforting in all its familiarity. His instructions were simple, even if difficult to actually apply when trying to find attraction to any one woman. But God never promised things would be easy, he reminded us.

The meeting ended in prayer, and several of us lingered for a little while afterwards. As we chatted, Mac stood close to me. I had wanted to talk to him for months, so I milked this opportunity for as long as I could edge us along in conversation.

"We should hang out sometime," I suggested to Mac and my fellow couch crew.

They all nodded, and Mac responded: "Oh yeah, definitely." I couldn't help but smirk.

✳

"You're fully engorged, eh?" I said, as Mac stood waist-high to his webcam, showing me his grey sweat-pant bulge.

"Yeah, I wonder why I'm so hard…" he replied. Though his face was hidden from the camera, I could hear the smile from the corner of his mouth curling his words.

"So strange! Random boners—you must still be going through puberty or something," I joked.

Mac and I had been Skyping for the past few weeks since I had returned to Toronto. We had decided to keep up while we were both away from Liberty for the summer. The distance between us let us operate as if what was between us wasn't actually real, that this was just fleeting fun, and what we were doing wasn't a big deal because it was only virtual. Besides, Mac and I never actually showed each other our bare dicks.

In fact, he and I never took our clothes off—with the exception of our shirts.

And, well, sometimes our shorts.

In other words, our underwear stayed on. *If we never saw what laid beneath, was it really all that bad?*

We would talk and talk and talk, and then when we would stand up or adjust our webcams, we would flash our bulges. We would pretend that it was an accident, but when the other would point out what he saw, we would then closely examine our erect cocks together, albeit cocks that were completely covered.

"It's harder than usual today."

"Why do you think that is?" I asked coyly.

"I think because I haven't looked at porn in almost three weeks," Mac responded matter-of-factly.

He didn't seem to pick up that I was still trying to flirt.

"Oh wow, yeah—that's awesome," I offered, shifting my tone to match his. Despite teasing each other on the regular, we nonetheless both still shared the belief that looking at porn was wrong and that we needed to spur each other on to godly living. It wasn't consistent thinking, but it was how we did things.

We were each other's accountability partner, but we had very little success in keeping each other sexually pure. The problem was that for us, we perpetually had sex on the brain—at least in part because we had no approved outlet for our libidos.

"I've never gotten to three weeks without masturbating. I always slip up and end up jerking off," I said.

"I still think about sex every day," Mac responded. But then he paused. He looked down at the corner of his screen, clearly in thought. "I honestly don't know how we're not supposed to masturbate until we get married. The more I try to ignore my dick, the more I can't get it out of my head. It just seems kinda impossible."

"I know what you mean. I just need to find a wife," I laughed.

During our Skype dates, the inevitable ebb and flow of showing the outlines of our hard penises and talking about God would ensue, where we would go back and forth between enticing each other and then discussing our need to remain pure. This push and pull defined these conversations, as it did much of our day-to-day lives.

"Yeah, same," Mac said.

In our world, wives were said to be the cure. Pastor Dane had told us that we didn't need to find *all* women attractive—just one woman would do. And when we found that woman, we needed to marry her—and it would be smooth sailing from there. We would still struggle with same-sex attraction, Dane said, but we would at least have an outlet for our hormones. A home for our dicks, as it were.

Mac continued, "Luke, do you remember when you said you wanted to hold my hand?"

"Yessir," I replied.

"I haven't stopped thinking about it since."

My stomach dropped.

"I want to know how your fingers feel around mine," he said before pausing again. Taking a deep breath in, he continued: "I want to know how big your hands are. If they're warm. Or if they're cold—I'd warm them up for you, if they were. I've never held hands with someone I actually want to hold hands with, and I just want to hold hands with you."

I stared at him as he leaned forward with his eyes looking down at his keyboard and his mouth slightly ajar, as if he wanted to tell me more. Instead, he looked up at me and closed his mouth, unsuccessfully trying to steady his bottom lip.

"Me too, Mac," I said.

I swallowed hard, still staring at him. His eyes were so handsome and so heavy—I wanted to kiss them closed, to let him rest and know that he was safe with me. "Even though I know it's wrong," I finally said, "at the end of the day I don't get why God is against us acting on our same-sex attractions. I really don't know why it's wrong to love a man."

"Are you saying you love me?" he laughed, pivoting quickly.

"No!" I smiled wide. "But what I *am* saying is that I want to hold your hand."

Mac's smile slowly faded, as his big eyes began to glaze over again. I kept staring at him, silently, watching him recede within himself. He looked tired.

"Well," he started. "I think it's time for me to go to work."

"Okay."

"Talk soon?"

"Of course," I said.

"Bye."

"Bye, mister."

✳

After that summer, I spoke with both Thad and Mac less and less. Thad moved out to Los Angeles after he graduated, as he said he would, where he finally came out and began to live that big gay lifestyle we had been warned about, the one we were told would lead to our spiritual, and potentially even to our physical, demise. Last I checked, Thad is still alive.

Though Mac and I remained friends for the remainder of the time we were both at Liberty, we never did end up pursuing anything beyond our Skype dates. And as with Thad, Mac and I eventually fell out of touch when we graduated. But a few years ago, when I went to look him up on Facebook, I found out that he had got married to—and now has a child with—a woman. I sometimes wonder if Mac, before he got married, ever got to hold hands with someone who wasn't his wife—someone whose hand he actually wanted to hold.

# AFTERWORD

I want to acknowledge that this collection has several representational shortcomings. As *Shame-Sex Attraction* focuses chiefly on stories of conversion practices in religious contexts, with the exception of one story, it is important to reiterate that conversion practices (and ideology) extend beyond religious organizations (and anti-LGBTQ2S+ religious biases).[1] Though conversion practices take place disproportionately at the hands of religious practitioners—overwhelmingly those who are Christian[2]—there is also a long history of change efforts in non-religious healthcare and counseling settings. Despite this recognition, this collection does not include stories about conversion therapy in such settings. Moreover, the vast majority of the contributors are white, though, as is noted above, research suggests that people of color are more likely to have been exposed to conversion practices. This lack of racial—in tandem

---

1    Jones, T. *et al.* (2022) "Religious conversion practices and LGBTQA+ youth." *Sexuality Research and Social Policy*, 19.

2    Burack, C. (2014) *Tough Love: Sexuality, Compassion, and the Christian Right.* Albany, NY: State University of New York Press; Salway, T. *et al.* (2019) "Protecting Canadian Sexual and Gender Minorities from Harmful Sexual Orientation and Gender Identity Change Efforts." A brief submitted to the Standing Committee on Health for the Committee's study of LGBTQ2 Health in Canada.

with geographical, religious, and ethnic—diversity thus does not speak to the wide range of communities that are subject to conversion practices. Regrettably, this collection also does not include stories by Two-Spirit folx, intersex individuals, Muslims, or those from the Global South. Although the stories by survivors from these communities—and by those who underwent conversion practices in non-religious healthcare and counseling settings—were sought and solicited, such submissions were not received, thereby limiting the representation possible in this collection. Another limitation is the title of the collection. Although the theme of "same-sex attraction" applies to the vast majority of contributors' stories, there is one story that does not refer to sexuality but instead focuses exclusively on gender identity and expression. I do not seek to eclipse this story and erase it by way of the volume's selected title. However, given how almost all the stories focus, at least in part, on sexual orientation, I have selected the title *Shame-Sex Attraction*, acknowledging that not every experience of conversion therapy in this collection (and beyond this collection) falls under the rubric of an exclusive effort to change individuals' sexualities.

# CONTRIBUTOR
# BIOGRAPHIES

**D. Apple** (she/her) is from Northern California and resides in the foothills of the Sierra Nevada mountains alongside her husband and their adventurous canine. Her journey started on a picnic table in the backyard of her childhood home. While conventional paths lead many to "support" groups or "therapists" for this kind of thing, Apple stubbornly believed in the power of dedicated homeschoolers to become straight, asserting that with sufficient effort, anyone can master the skills they need—or think they need—to do so. Armed with a B.S. in Graphic Design from Sacramento State University, Apple applies her need for both right- and left-brain activities as a designer in a local print shop, in addition to indulging in her passion for reading and writing. Her happy place is cozying up on the couch with her dog and a 19th-century Gothic mystery novel, but you'll also find her hiking and exploring ghost towns and forgotten graveyards with her husband. She is currently in the final stages of editing her first historical novel.

**Lexie Bean** (they/he) is a trans multimedia artist from the Midwest whose work revolves around themes of bodies, homes, cyclical violence, and queer identity. They are a Jerome Hill Artist Fellow, a member of the RAINN National Leadership Council, and a Lambda

Literary Award Finalist for their anthology *Written on the Body*. Bean integrated their personal experiences into the acclaimed *The Ship We Built* (Dial Books, 2021), the first middle-grade novel centering on and written by a trans boy released by a major U.S. publisher. Their work has been featured in *Teen Vogue*, *The New York Times*, *The Huffington Post*, *The Feminist Wire*, *Ms. Magazine*, *Them*, *Bust Magazine*, *Autostraddle*, as well as Jessica Kingsley Publishers' *Surviving Transphobia*. Currently they are working on new book projects, film writing, and co-directing their first feature-length documentary, *What Will I Become?*

**Colin Bland** (they/them) is originally from South Carolina, where they attended Clemson University and earned a B.A. in Architecture and an M.Arch. Bland was involved in conservative Christian traditions from early childhood through early adulthood, eventually breaking free from harmful ideas in search of LGBTQ2S+ liberation. Bland underwent conversion therapy in 2010 as a minor and again as a young adult while in undergrad (2015–2017) at the hands of pastoral staff members employed by a local church in the Southern Baptist Convention. Bland married their long-term partner, Anthony, in 2023, and the two now enjoy traveling together and spoiling their pet husky, Sasha.

**Garrard Conley** (he/him) is the author of his memoir *Boy Erased* (Penguin, 2016), a *New York Times* bestseller and now a major motion picture. *Boy Erased* was nominated for a Lambda Literary Award and was featured as a top 2016 nonfiction book by *O Magazine*, *BuzzFeed Books*, and *Shelf Awareness*, among others. It has now been translated in over a dozen languages. More recently, he has published *All the World Beside* (Riverhead/Penguin, 2024), a novel about the love story between two men in Puritan New England. His other work can be found in *The New York Times, The Independent, The Oxford American, TIME, VICE, CNN, BuzzFeed, Them, Virginia Quarterly Review, Joyland Magazine, The Florida Review*, and *The Huffington Post*, among other venues. He is also a producer and creator of the podcast *UnErased*. He has received scholarships from MacDowell, Bread Loaf, Sewanee, the Studios of Key West, Virginia Center for the Creative Arts, and the Elizabeth Kostova Foundation Writers' Conferences and has taught writing classes for Catapult, Sackett Street Writers Workshop, and the Fine Arts Works Center in Provincetown. He is a member of the PEN/America Foundation and serves on the board of the Mattachine Society of Washington, D.C. He holds an M.F.A. in Creative Writing from Brooklyn College, as well as an M.A. in English from Auburn University. Conley is an Assistant Professor of Creative Writing at Kennesaw State University.

**Chris Csabs** (he/him) is a survivor of conversion practices that took place between the ages of 16 and 23. He is co-founder of the Australian survivor advocacy group SOGICE Survivors and co-author of the "SOGICE Survivor Statement," a document that has been utilized by advocates, researchers, and policy-writers in Australia and around the world. Csabs is a leading voice in the campaign to see Australian governments take action, with three Australian states and territories passing legislation to combat conversion practices and several others committing to do so. SOGICE Survivors won the 2021 Victorian Pride Award for Community Inspiration following their contribution to the successful passage of Victoria's Change or Suppression Practices Prohibition Act, which has been recognized as being among the most comprehensive pieces of legislation that prohibits conversion practices in the world. Csabs has been at the forefront of Australian media surrounding the issue of conversion practices, on television (including on *Christians Like Us, Today,*

*The Feed*, and *The Project*), radio, and a variety of podcasts. He is a respected LGBTQ2S+ advocate, having presented at conferences and authored a range of media articles about conversion practices in Australia.

**Rick Danielson** (he/him) is from western New York, where he attended Houghton University before attaining M.Div. and D.Min. degrees from Asbury Theological Seminary in Kentucky. Prior to retiring from Community United Church of Christ in Boulder, Colorado, he served as a pastor in the United Methodist and United Church of Christ denominations in New York and Maine. He and his husband Leroy Lewis ran a bed and breakfast inn in the Finger Lakes region of New York and currently live in Buffalo. Danielson underwent episodic conversion therapy from 1983–2002.

**Gregory Elsasser-Chavez** (he/him) lives and teaches high-school English in Los Angeles, California, where he also lives with his husband. He is a father of three boys and a published playwright of eight plays, one novel, and his memoir, *Terms of Estrangement* (Austin Macauley Publishers, 2023), a book of letters written to his son detailing his coming-out process and full 25-year conversion therapy experience.

**Gemma Hickey** (they/them) is a multi-award winning international author, human rights advocate, and global speaker from Newfoundland and Labrador. Their advocacy has made headlines worldwide and changed the legal landscape of Canada, expanding the rights, dignity, and equality of women, LGBTQ2S+ communities, and survivors of religious institutional abuse. Hickey's highly acclaimed memoir, *Almost Feral* (Breakwater, 2019), chronicles their 938-kilometre trek across Newfoundland and the uncharted emotional landscapes within. In 2023, they were honored with the Governor General's Award in Commemoration of the Persons Case.

**Kim Kemmis** (he/him) is a writer, activist, and historian from Sydney, New South Wales, Australia. After entering the ministry in a conservative evangelical church, he went through conversion therapy at Liberty Christian Ministries. He holds a Ph.D. in History from the University of Sydney and researches Australian cultural history and the history of bisexuality. When he is not writing academic articles or fiction, he is usually playing classical guitar.

**Syre Klenke** (he/him) is a trans activist based in Los Angeles, California. He is a writer and marketing consultant. He spends his free time participating in both digital and in-person activism to ensure LGBTQ2S+ communities in the U.S. finally receive equal rights, especially those who are members of other marginalized communities. He loves to write, create art, and spend time outdoors. He hopes that his story can help prevent other individuals from going through so-called conversion therapy, especially youth. While the piece shared in this book is from an experience in 2009, Klenke's experience of being forced to attend so-called conversion therapy by his parents did not start there. This is a driving factor in his activism and determination to end conversion therapy around the world.

**Tyler Krumland** (he/him) was raised in Olympia, Washington. He took part in an online form of conversion therapy called Setting Captives Free. He holds a B.A. in Communications from North Park University and an M.A. in Christian Formation from North Park Theological Seminary. He is a former youth pastor who now works in healthcare. In the spring of 2020, he published his memoir *Love Him Well: My Journey Towards God, Truth, and Self-Acceptance* (independently published), which covers his journey growing up as a closeted evangelical and how he came to embrace being gay. He is a writer, an occasional speaker, and an artist. He currently lives in Portland, Oregon, with his two dogs.

**Chaim Levin** (he/him) grew up in a Hasidic sect of the Jewish community in Brooklyn, New York. He holds a B.A. in Television and Radio from Brooklyn College. When he was 18, he underwent conversion therapy for a year and a half through a now defunct organization called Jews Offering New Alternatives to Homosexuality, better known as JONAH. At the age of 23, Levin and five others became the first group of people to ever successfully pursue a lawsuit against a conversion therapy organization in the U.S. *Ferguson v. JONAH* resulted in the closure of JONAH on the grounds that it committed consumer fraud by selling a product that was inherently fraudulent. Levin has written extensively about his experiences in conversion therapy in various publications, including *The Huffington Post*. Most recently he appeared in a short film, entitled "'It's Still an Emergency': The Vulnerability of Queer Orthodox Jews," published by *The New York Times*, about his experiences growing up in a very religious community as a gay man.

**Peter Nunn** (he/him) lives with his husband Monte in Atlanta, Georgia, about an hour from his childhood home. He owns and operates a hair salon and serves as a board member and public policy chair for the American Foundation for Suicide Prevention—Georgia Chapter. Nunn has had the chance to advocate for conversion therapy bans at state capitals, the U.S. Capitol, and in media interviews with the Apple+ show *Dear...*, National Public Radio, *Playboy Magazine*, and others. He and his mother have become much closer in the years following his coming out, and she attended Peter and Monte's wedding in 2014. Over

20 years after his attempted suicide, Peter is living the life that he was told by conversion therapists he could never have, which includes being healthy, loved, and successful. He uses his story and his voice to help make sure that others don't have to go through the same things he did.

**Megan Poirier** (she/her) is from Boston, Massachusetts, though she has previously lived in both Maine and Texas. She was raised in an evangelical church and briefly underwent conversion efforts through their ex-gay ministry as a teenager. She has a B.A. in Political Science with a minor in Creative Writing from the University of Maine at Farmington. She currently resides in south-eastern Massachusetts, where she works as a library technician. She enjoys reading, playing video games, and spending time with her friends and her cat Lovey.

**Jonathon Sawyer** (he/him) was raised in Albuquerque, New Mexico, and resides in Boulder, Colorado. After graduating from high school, Sawyer enrolled in Spirit Life Bible College (SLBC), a now defunct independent charismatic Christian school in southern California that was affiliated with a network known as the New Apostolic Reformation. At SLBC, he experienced various forms of conversion therapy. He holds a B.A.A.S. in Music, History, and Religion from the University of North Texas, and an M.A. in Education from the University of Colorado Boulder. He is now a Ph.D. candidate working with the National Education Policy Center at the University of Colorado Boulder. His dissertation examines the religion clauses of the First Amendment and the constitutional rights of LGBTQ 2S+ students in religious schools. He has written on the conspiratorial and anti-LGBTQ 2S+ teachings and practices of the New Apostolic Reformation in *Review of Education, Pedagogy, and Cultural Studies* (forthcoming). He has also published in *HuffPost* and was featured in a two-part series on the *IndoctriNation* podcast.

**Jordan Sullivan** (he/him) is a queerly heterosexual trans man, born and raised in Ottawa, Ontario, Canada. He has lived in Alberta, California, and the Marshall Islands (Micronesia), and he now lives in Toronto. He is a survivor of religious-based conversion "therapy" practices that he internalized for decades and formally experienced in Oshawa, Ontario. Jordan is the SOGIECE/CP Prevention and Survivor Support Coordinator at the Community-Based Research Centre where he led the SOGIECE/CT Survivor Support Project, created the website https://stopconversionpractices.ca, along with a learning module on conversion "therapy" practices in Canada. He is currently coordinating an intersectoral project (2024–2025) to establish a Canadian coalition on ending conversion practices. He co-authored a chapter in *Banning Conversion Therapy: Legal and Policy Perspectives* and has been interviewed by *Xtra Magazine, CBC Halifax, Global Morning News, CanQueer Radio,* and *Queer FM Radio*. Sullivan has worked as an elementary school teacher, in public education for the Canadian Mental Health Association, and in various capacities including LGBTQ2S+ Justice for The United Church of Canada. He has a B.A. Sc. in Elementary Education from Weimar College and an M.A. in Religious Studies from La Sierra University.

**Lucas F. W. Wilson** (he/him) formerly the Justice, Equity, and Transformation Postdoctoral Fellow at the University of Calgary, is a Social Sciences and Humanities Research Council Postdoctoral Fellow at the University of Toronto Mississauga. His public-facing work has appeared in *The Advocate, Queerty, LGBTQ Nation,* and *Religion Dispatches,* among other venues. His academic work has appeared in *Modern Language Studies, Flannery O'Connor Review, Canadian Jewish Studies, Journal of Jewish Identities,* and *Studies in American Jewish Literature,* and in edited collections published by The MLA, SUNY Press, The University of Alabama Press, and DIO Press. He is the author of *At Home with the Holocaust: Postmemory, Domestic Space, and Second-Generation Holocaust Narratives* (Rutgers University Press, 2025)—for which he won the Association for Jewish Studies' Jordan Schnitzer First Book Publication Award—and the co-editor of *Emerging Trends in Third-Generation Holocaust Literature* (Lexington Books, 2023).

**Nathan Xie** (he/they) is a writer from Connecticut. He is a recipient of One Story's Adina Talve-Goodman Fellowship and he has been supported by Lambda Literary, the Periplus Collective, and Tin House. His writing appears or is forthcoming in *The Southern Review*, *New England Review*, *The Rumpus*, and more.